Lifelines

Books by Philip Booth

Pairs

Selves

Relations

Before Sleep

Available Light

Margins

Weathers and Edges

The Islanders

Letter from a Distant Land

PHILIP BOOTH

Lifelines

SELECTED POEMS

1950–1999

VIKING

VIKING
Published by the Penguin Group
Penguin Putnam Inc., 375 Hudson Street, New York, New York 10014, U.S.A.
Penguin Books Ltd, 27 Wrights Lane, London W8 5TZ, England
Penguin Books Australia Ltd, Ringwood, Victoria, Australia
Penguin Books Canada Ltd, 10 Alcorn Avenue, Toronto, Ontario, Canada M4V 3B2
Penguin Books (N.Z.) Ltd, 182–190 Wairau Road, Auckland 10, New Zealand

Penguin Books Ltd, Registered Offices: Harmondsworth, Middlesex, England

First published in 1999 by Viking Penguin, a member of Penguin Putnam Inc.

10 9 8 7 6 5 4 3 2 1

The poems in Sections I–IX of this volume originally appeared in *The American Poetry Review*, *American Scholar*, *Antaeus*, *The Atlantic Monthly*, *The Beloit Poetry Journal*, *Choomia*, *The Country Journal*, *Field*, *The Georgia Review*, *Harper's*, *Harvard Magazine*, *The Hudson Review*, *Ironwood*, *Kayak*, *The Kenyon Review*, *London Magazine*, *The Missouri Review*, *The Nation*, *The New England Review*, *New Orleans Poetry Journal*, *The New Republic*, *The New York Review of Books*, *The New Yorker*, *North Dakota Quarterly*, *The Ohio Review*, *The Ontario Review*, *The Palaemon Press*, *Pequod*, *Poetry*, *Poetry Northwest*, *Princeton University Library Chronicle*, *River Styx*, *Salmagundi*, *Saturday Review*, *Shenandoah*, *Tendril*, *TriQuarterly*, *The Virginia Quarterly Review*, *The Yale Review*, and in the author's earlier books *Letter from a Distant Land*, *The Islanders*, *Weathers and Edges*, *Margins*, *Available Light*, *Before Sleep*, *Relations*, and *Selves* published by Viking Penguin and *Pairs*, published by Penguin Books.

Page 292 constitutes an extension of this copyright page.

LIBRARY OF CONGRESS CATALOGING-IN-PUBLICATION DATA
Booth, Philip E.
    Lifelines : selected poems, 1950–1999 / Philip Booth.
      p.   cm.
    ISBN 0-670-88287-9
    I. Title.
    PS3552.O647A6   1999   98–46250
    811'.54—dc21

This book is printed on acid-free paper. ∞

Printed in the United States of America
Set in ITC Garamond
Designed by Betty Lew

CONTENTS

Lifelines

*1) Safety lines supported by
stanchions along the rails
of a sizeable pleasure boat.*

*2) Small lines thrown to
retrieve someone fallen
overboard, or in danger of
drowning.*

*3) Lines diagonally crossing the
palm of a human hand, believed
to signify the major events and
the length of one's life.*

I

NIGHTSONG

Beside you,
lying down at dark,
my waking fits your sleep.

Your turning
flares the slow-banked fire
between our mingled feet,

and there,
curved close and warm
against the nape of love,

held there,
who holds your dreaming
shape, I match my breathing

to your breath;
and sightless, keep my hand
on your heart's breast, keep

nightwatch
on your sleep to prove
there is no dark, nor death.

FIRST LESSON

Lie back, daughter, let your head
be tipped back in the cup of my hand.
Gently, and I will hold you. Spread
your arms wide, lie out on the stream
and look high at the gulls. A dead-
man's-float is face down. You will dive
and swim soon enough where this tidewater
ebbs to the sea. Daughter, believe
me, when you tire on the long thrash
to your island, lie up, and survive.
As you float now, where I held you
and let go, remember when fear
cramps your heart what I told you:
lie gently and wide to the light-year
stars, lie back, and the sea will hold you.

SHAG

Under the slow heron,
flip tern, and swung gull,
six black shags run on
the water, each duck skull

filled with weathervane
thought. Toward East wind
they take off on the run,
splashing until the shag mind

tells spent feet to retract.
Then the seventh shag,
straggling, begins to react.
His head bobs. The fog

closing in, he raises
himself on gargoyle wings,
drops again, then rises
and runs as he bangs

the sea on all fours.
Slowly, then faster, he skims
the dark fir shores.
Momentarily, he seems

to join the first flight.
But he shoots away,
shaglike, his thought flat
black. All shags fly

low. Ornithologists know
more: the perhaps why
and improbable how
of shag flight. They

call them cormorants,
or latinize the North name.
I row slow in the dense
weather. This is Maine;

and I slap the split port oar
of my leaking skiff,
drifting among the fir
islands, the seabirds, as if

on vacation from knowledge:
six black shags, shagging;
August fog, me, a Maine ledge,
and the seventh shag, lagging.

CHART 1203
Penobscot Bay and Approaches

Whoever works a storm to windward, sails
in rain, or navigates in island fog,
must reckon from the slow swung lead, from squalls

on cheek; must bear by compass, chart, and log.
Parallels are ruled from compass rose
to known red nun: but still the landfall leg

risks set of tide, lost buoys, and breakers' noise
on shore where no shore was. Whoever plots
his homing on these Eastward islands knows

how Sou'west smoke obscures the sunny charts,
how gulls cry on a numberless black spar.
Where North is West of North, not true, he pilots

best who feels the coast for standpipe, spire,
tower, or stack, who owns local knowledge of shoal
or ledge, whose salt nose smells the spruce shore.

Where echoes drift, where the blind groundswell
clangs an iron bell, his fish-hook hand
keeps steady on the helm. He weathers rainsquall,

linestorm, fear, who bears away from the sound
of sirens wooing him to the cape's safe lee.
He knows the ghostship bow, the sudden headland

immanent in fog; but where rocks wander, he
steers down the channel that his courage
dredges. He knows the chart is not the sea.

STORM IN A FORMAL GARDEN

Where my struck mother stays,
she wakes to thunderstorms
of doubt. Squalls blacken
her bright-surfaced dreams,
and she stands coldly shaken,
lost in the dripping trees.

The weather shuts and opens:
horizon lightning traps
her in a quick exposure
of old fears; she trips
and rises twice unsure.
No one knows how it happens.

Where my dark mother waits
for sun, the wet slate sky
builds prison thunderheads,
and she, mired in anxiety,
must bear the drumroll nights
struck mute by what she dreads.

Her numb-mouthed silences
are desperate prayer, or else
the panic count from flash
to thunderclap. Impulse
fires her woman flesh,
and fevers her thin balances.

Miles from where my mother
falls, in that rank formal
garden that I bend

to weed, the wrens chirp normal
pleasure on the wind,
wrens scale the turning weather.

Weeds like conscience clog
my rake. My mother craves
more love than any son
can give. And I, with leaves
jammed on a sharpened tine,
sweat where my two hearts tug.

Dreams from her, I wake
beyond my mother's hope
and will. Beyond the son
I was, and the thunder's shape,
I clear the overgrown
last path my heart must rake.

LETTER FROM A DISTANT LAND

I, on my side, require of every writer,
first or last, a simple and sincere
account of his own life . . . some such
account as he would send to his
kindred from a distant land. . . .
                          —Thoreau, *Walden*

Henry, my distant kin,
                      I live halfway,
halfway between an airfield and your pond,
halfway within the house I moved to buy
by borrowing. On transcendental ground,
come South from colder hills and early dusk,
we claim two acres of uneven land.
Alone now, sitting at my birch-plank desk,
I see an acre out these wide new windows:
my wife cuts brush, two small girls both risk
a foot in appletrees. Across the meadows,
the alder swamp, an ash grove not yet green,
a pair of jets outrace their double shadows.
We do not look up. A grosbeak in the pine
pecks under wing, the shy hen pheasant leaves
her nibbled sumac for our scattered grain.
With rabbits, too, we share uncertain lives;
not quiet or desperate, we measure man
by how he lives and what he most believes.
I am half teacher, half-week chopping blow-down
for our fire, half-time professing words
to warm new minds with what my heart has known.
My classes are good failures. Afterwards,
I change clothes, moult my partial self,
and walk completed through the open woods.

Behind the grillwork branches where I half
confess, the chapel that I most attend
is choired by migratory birds; I loaf
within the absolution of the wind.
My thought is swiftest when my feet are slow,
but far abroad I own a spendthrift mind.
My Spanish grandfather, a tall man, knew
his knighthood from a book. So, pastoral
beside a fire, do I come slowly to know
you, odd uncle of my wakeful, still,
and secret dawns. My least experiments
with seed, like yours with a dried apple, fail;
the weeds, slugs, borers, grow as dense
as crows. I own a herd dog, but no sheep;
my cultivation is, like learning, chance.
Slack puritan I am, I let my garden shape
itself with skunks. I'm halfway, halfway only;
there are midnights when I do not sleep.

The quick night-fighters' sudden thunder shakes
this house awake. Escaped from every weather,
making prey of man, they are great sharks
with silver fins that foul the ocean air.
Propelled by jets of flame fired through their vents,
they school a noisy mile Northeast of here,
guided by blind pilots, and by governments.
A war ago, I flew myself. Now, bound
to these two acres, I owe the several debts
a lonely conscience knows. I love this land
by the salt sweat it costs to own it whole.
My birthday was a bucksaw, I still defend
the new growth with an ax: the trees I fell
need cutting to let the hardwood grow. I chop
at the lush swamp, hack down the summer jungle
rich with flies. You know how fires earned chip

by chip are warmest. Still, you could not guess
the shapes of proved destruction: chain saws rape
a virgin stand to stumps; raw foremen boss
more horsepower in a fleet of airfield trucks
than Concord ever stabled. Machines as murderous
as mad bulls gore the land. Where stacked cornshocks
stood last fall, an orange oil tank flaws
the spring; girders bloom with concrete blocks.
So far, your Concord has seen four more wars.
Vegetables are high. The streets are filled
with tourists; cheap people in expensive cars
patrol the Sunday roads. An acre sold
in 1849 sells now two hundred times
the price. Lexington is houses sprawled
on desert-dusty streets with fertile names.
The arrogant inherit lust. Everywhere,
thick rows of sportsmen fish polluted streams,
or hunt the posted woods of their own fear.
Overhead, the tight-paired jets write
cryptic warnings on the thin blue air.

Too close to earth to show to those who scan
the sky for enemy, I walked last week
beyond the impulse caught on any radar screen.
In windworn March, halfway to dawn, I woke
to feel the growing day: the wind light North-
north-west, the morning luminous, a streak
of cloud between the sunward-turning earth
and yesterday's last stars. A rebel drummer
called me like the crows. The cross-lots path
I walked was wet with melting frost, a rumor
of frogs thawed the swamp, and toward town
I heard the hard first whack of a hammer.
A casual pilgrim to the phoebe's tune,
I whistled down the distant land where you

(this same month's end) tramped out to cut white pine
with Alcott's borrowed ax. Your Walden, now,
is still half yours: a summer swimmers' beach
corrupts the eastern bank, the sunup view,
but you, who would be saint in a formal church,
are honored still on the farther shores, preserved
in the commonwealth of hemlock, elm, and birch.
Your hut is marked by stone, the pond was saved
by taxes for a public park. Emerson's
strict laws of compensation have reserved
a parking space for Sunday lovers; beer cans
drift where you knelt soberly to drink,
and small boys smoke like truant puritans.
Such is August on the swimmers' bank,
but not my sharp March dawn. Between ice-out
and spring, I walk in time to hear the honk
of two stray geese, the song of a white-throat
soloing after his mate in your celibate woods.
That song is still the same; shadowy trout
rise like the swift perfection of your words,
the backyard journal of your human praise
is proved in the red oaks' blood-dark buds.
I like to think how animals would freeze
to see your stick, your crooked genius, poke
the leafy underbrush: until you froze
yourself, and all the thicket woodcock, duck,
and small scared beasts of Walden's shore
turned curious. Here, between the dark
and sudden milktrain day, halfway from fear,
halfway to spring, I say these natural names
to honor you as poet of the turning year.
Beside the ministry of waves, the times
of men are seasons, windfall seeds that spill
toward fruit: the perfect globe or wormy shames
of Adam. All poets climb back Eden's hill

within their own backyard. Woods and pond
were your recovery of the crop that's possible,
a harvest of good words grown from the land
that brings the whole world home. I cultivate
a different orchard, pruning under the sound
of probable war. The day's first silver jet
reflects first sunlight where I turn away
from Walden, turn, stop, look back, and start
again. Up the bank, I cross the highway
where a skunk got lost in headlights: traffic-
flat, his flowering intestines lie halfway
in sun. This new March day is sweetened thick
with death. But when was any season less?
You felt the cold fall snap of John Brown's neck,
owned a winter conscience, smelled slavery's grass-
fire torch the long dry land to civil war,
from Bull Run to Savannah to the Wilderness.
Distant from that history as we are,
the good, the brave, are no more a majority
than when you walked this far spring shore.
Man, by his human nature, is not free;
but where his wildness is alive to swamp
and hill, he learns to live most naturally.
Still, a saunterer must make his camp
in strange unholy lands, begging alms
and passage for belief. I take no stump
except for liberty to listen to the elms,
to walk the cold wood, to sleep on bedrock
thought, and to try some winter psalms.
A century from where your wisdom struck
its temporary camp, I cross the middleground
toward hope. At home beneath both oak
and jet, praising what I halfway understand,
I walk this good March morning out
to say my strange love in a distant land.

II

THE SECOND NOON

New to light that first noon,
they stand blind in the sun's meridian,
and own no sight, but hang their heads down
from that glare and first heat
until, as the day grows cool,
their accustomed eyes can open,
and they recognize the original shadows
leaning out from their feet.

Asking that afternoon nothing,
they worship those doubled forms who swim
before them onto the streaming meadows.
Grown tall at last to turn
questions, they face behind them,
full West, and—stumbling blind
beyond guesses of dawn—are pressed
into the aggregate shadows.

They wake to a slivered moon
that first night, to a sky wet with stars,
and in that world cannot believe
they see. And will not see
(as light from love revolves)
until, as their shadows come home
foot by foot, they learn to look not to the sun,
but full, at high noon, to themselves.

WAS A MAN

Was a man, was a two-
faced man, pretended
he wasn't who he was,
who, in a men's room,
faced his hung-over
face in a mirror hung
over the towel rack.
The mirror was cracked.
Shaving close in that
looking glass, he nicked
his throat, bled blue
blood, grabbed a new
towel to patch the wrong
scratch, knocked off
the mirror and, facing
himself, almost intact,
in final terror hung
the wrong face back.

THESE MEN

for M.V.D.

What is man, that mindful of him
in his last act, I let tears blind me?
Scene after scene, his voice
is his sword's, yet when chaste stars illumine
his justice, his choice
is finally to fall from the height his words
must reach. These men remind me.

Not that through their thin mask I name
them, walking on in crossed light, or pray
to a stage that time will revolve.
Too frail to be gods, men who need women
and silence, who love
to be loved, they risk their trial words
to redeem not themselves but the play.

Speaking, they speak cast out of time:
a prince who would break up the dumb-show,
a kingdom-dividing king, a son
at the crossroads; they question how common
it is to be man,
and measured for death by their words'
grave rise, sentence themselves to know.

THE TOWER

Strangers ask,
always, how tall
it is. Taller,
the natives say,
than any other.
Watching it sway,
lightly, in a brisk
wind, you believe
them and feel,
well, smaller
than you once
did, or would have,
even had they woken
somebody's father,
who remembers
every specification,
they say, having fought
against this location,
in the last elections
before it was built.
It is enough
to see it, canted
over you, as
you approach
the strange base:
a cement stilt
set in a rough
patch of marsh;
on that, a ball
with numbers
etched on it,

perhaps a date,
on which the steel
frame, in one
brave unbroken
line, seems to stretch
for heaven itself,
in three diminishing
sections. The balance
is fantastic,
or seems so, until
you recall the elastic
web of guy wires
that, slanted
beyond you, support
the tower in nine
equal directions
The local women,
hanging their wash
on a wet line,
Monday, report
that it's hidden
in clouds, out
of mind, until,
in a sudden
wind and vanishing
fog, they look up:
not to worship
but, more, from habit;
the way, once left
home when their men
went to rivet
the thing, they said
morning prayers.
Even on Sunday,
now, of course,

they accept how
the shadow swings
down, leaning
in and away
in elliptic rings
like a sundial.
Or so a high
state official
told them it did,
when they, craning
that broken sky,
sat assembled
there for the long
dedication:
it resembled,
he said, nothing
so much; and laughing
then, said if you
knew where you were
(they laughed too),
and perhaps how far
from the solstice,
you could almost tell
what time it was,
by when the shadow
fell on your house.
Not that the tower
itself would fall,
ever, on such
a quiet meadow
of homes, nor would
the isogonic reaction
affect, even touch,
their elm trees;
the theta conductors

were shielded, at
his personal direction,
he said, so not
to entail any risk
for them, or their families.
A man, then, stood
tall, as if to ask
a first question, but
near him a guard
preserved order.
There was, the speaker
admitted, an odor
caused by the breaker
circuits, but this
was the new power,
in essence, and, as
designed, wouldn't last.
A solar device,
he called it, strong
as the Nation
itself, which, because
of such structures,
would stand until
Kingdom Come.
They were proud there,
then; and still are,
when their children,
or children's children,
home from municipal
lectures, recite,
without prompting,
the smallest detail:
the interval
of each warning light,
and how, just

at dawn, the strange
orange glow
on top will go
out, with something
suspended, like
lazing snow
in the morning air;
not much, a flake
here, a flake there,
which dissolves
to a kind of dust
that settles, daily,
around the globular
base. And, daily,
the child who puts up
the flag is assigned,
also, to sweep.
Once every year
they make wreaths
(of jagged cut felt,
shaped like elm leaves)
and lay them here,
between the new sidewalk
and Main Street.
Otherwise, nothing
is changed: home
is the same, talk
still revolves
around the same
people. Government
studies, given
every control,
have proven
this. The report
is unanimous,

to every intent:
there's been neither
famine nor war.
Their original
fear of the fall
is gone, the range
of the shadow
seems less, the weather
more clear. The meadows
are full of new flowers;
stakes are aligned
on most lawns, shaped
like sundials.
Women count hours
still; they repeat
household trials,
and gossip. But
except for
the fool who tried
climbing the tower,
few have died;
most have escaped
the usual town
diseases; misbegotten
children are
fewer, the suicide
rate is down.
Indeed, nothing
is ominous
here, unless
you take stock
of their dreams:
waking, sometimes,
they say, it hangs
over them: not

exactly the tower
itself, but what
they've forgotten,
something above
the tower, like
a dance tune
they can't quite
remember, or name.
They are used to
the circuit breakers
now; they admit
it, even to
government
census-takers,
who wake them—
women weeping
over their sleeping
men, at dawn—
since only then,
before day
begins, will they
try to show,
without words,
but pointing towards
the tower, that what
they can't name
is, like waking
itself, or making
love, not different,
no, but in spite
of the Government,
yes, not quite
the same.

SEA-CHANGE

John Marin
(1870–1953)

Marin
saw how it feels:
the first raw shock
of Labrador current,
the surfacing gasp
at jut of rock,
bent sails, and wedged
trees. He wrote it:
Stonington, Small
Point, and Cape Split,
through a pane so
cracked by the lode-
star sun that he
swam back, blinded,
into himself to
sign the after-
image: initialed
mountains, ledged
towns (white as
Machias after
the hayrake rain),
sun-splintered
water and written
granite; dark light
unlike what you
ever saw until,
inland, your own
eyes close and, out
of that sea-change,

islands rise thick:
like the rip-tide
paint that, flooding,
tugs at your vitals,
and is more Maine
than Maine.

THE ISLANDERS

Winters when we set our traps offshore
we saw an island further out than ours,
miraged in midday haze, but lifting clear
at dawn, or late flat light, in cliffs that might
have been sheer ice. It seemed, then, so near,

that each man, turning home with his slim catch,
made promises beyond the limits of his gear
and boat. But mornings we cast off to watch
the memory blur as we attempted it,
and set and hauled on ledges we could fetch

and still come home. Summers, when we washed
inshore again, not one of us would say
the island's name, though none at anchor sloshed
the gurry from his deck without one eye
on that magnetic course the ospreys fished.

Winters, then, we knew which way to steer
beyond marked charts, and saw the island as
first islanders first saw it: who watched it blur
at noon, yet harbored knowing it was real;
and fished, like us, offshore, as if it were.

III

THE DAY THE TIDE

The day the tide went out,
and stayed, not just at Mean
Low Water or Spring Ebb,
but out, out all the way
perhaps as far as Spain,
until the bay was empty,

it left us looking down
at what the sea, and our
reflections on it, had
(for generations of
good fish, and wives fair
as vessels) saved us from.

We watched our fishboats ground
themselves, limp-chained in mud;
careened, as we still are
(though they lie far below us)
against this sudden slope
that once looked like a harbor.

We're level, still, with islands,
or what's still left of them
now that treelines invert:
the basin foothills rock
into view like defeated castles,
with green and a flagpole on top.

Awkward as faith itself,
heron still stand on one leg
in trenches the old tide cut;

maybe they know what the moon's
about, working its gravity
off the Atlantic shelf.

Blind as starfish, we
look into our dried reservoir
of disaster: fouled trawls, old
ships hung up on their mon-
ument ribs; the skeletons
of which our fathers were master.

We salt such bones down with self-
consolation, left to survive,
if we will, on this emptied slope.
Réunion Radio keeps reporting
how our ebb finally flooded
the terrible Cape of Good Hope.

FAIRY TALE

Half awake, the boy in the big bed haunted
by guns sits up to fire his blank tears.
The world he dreamed was a palace, painted
blue to match the Queen's dress. There were fairs
every day. He could swim. Whenever he wanted

the animals left, and a tent slanted
over the chair where he kept her warm.
Because of the dwarf in the moat, he invented
the gun she let him have; he guarded her room
at night. Whatever he asked, she granted.

He lived there years and years: he counted
time by counting how many names
he could find for that dark, dwarf-stunted,
man in the moat, and how many times
he had killed what all those names hunted.

He dreamed all this. He dreamed that scented
Queen who'd never, ever, let him be dead.
But when he woke, he could hear, tented
over her, big as the dark of her bed,
the dwarf whose black cannon was mounted.

His fingers wanted to kill, but were blunted
with lead: a world of infinite corridors
weighted his waking, and everywhere slanted
away, away from dreaming to wars
in bed; which was not the world he wanted.

CLEANING OUT THE GARAGE
for J.B.F.

Hooks, screw-eyes, and screws; the walls
thick with bent nails to catch on: somebody's
grandfather must have hoped his grandson
would use these nicked tools. Adze, spoke-shave,
and saw hang with dead moth-wings, spidered
to leaning studs. Fifty winters have heaved
this catch-all off its foundations, cracked
the poured-floor, and left to mildew the tent
I almost slept in, moored to my boyhood backyard.

Sponges that bilged three lapstrake rowboats
(the lot of them rotted or sunk) stiffen
like pockmarked soft footballs; instructions
for washing the Model-T Ford curl tacked
to the faucet plank. The wall is shelved
with paintcans left to weather, their paint
skinned like my grandfather's wrinkles. The gloss
has gone soft on his set of golf clubs: troon,
nap-iron, and niblick, bagged with balls but no
putter, their hickory shafts still true.

It's summer when I haul back to all this:
a goldfinch dead in a box of unplanted
seeds, chemicals bagged to poison the weeds
that still flourish. Stormed by the dust
of my sweeping, storm windows lean stacked
like the panes my boyhood couldn't see through.
I try to sweep out the useless stuff I still
cherish: a drugstore sloop that tipped over,
a bathtub submarine that floated between

my legs like a small sick fish; I try not
to sink in this scrap I dive to uncover.

Cars jacked up here, in '18 and '43,
the Ford and a Chevy, still stain the cracked floor
with drip from their oilpans; my great-
grandfather's (substitute's) Civil War sword
points North like the rusted compass my family
never trusted: in all the winters somebody
shoveled a path to this island garage,
there was gear for voyages, wars, or rebuilding;
enough to see whole generations through.
I'm game for different winters in this high summer;
a woman I loved who refused me taught me what I
mean to leave here: how to let go what won't do.

DENYING THE DAY'S MILE

Always on clear mornings
I wake across their valley
to face the day's horizon:
quickened by my tentative
steps, I leap it like
the solo shadow of a big
jet—behind which I
am the sun.
                    By the time
dusk takes my neighbor's
streetcorner, and staggers
me home, I'm overcast
always: I imagine men
in the Andaman Islands
waking to fish, women
giving breast in Lhasa
to children the color of rice.
But I can never conceive
what weather they wake to, or
face those multiple hands
that bait my eye to a map.
I've never even been sure
whether they're still beginning
a day I've already lost,
or a day I haven't begun.
Even with my ear close
as a child's to waves
bounced off Afghanistan,
the Black Sea, and London,
there is too much static
to pick up children eating

fists of Tibetan snow.
Before God died, I thought
it might be fun to try
his game for a while: not
to judge the world, but simply
to listen in on how
it was getting on. Now
I couldn't bear it: I can't
even stand my neighbors,
or face myself when I go
to bed with no love left
from the day.
                    Always on clear
mornings I wake intending
to walk a mile, and to hold
that mile's particulars up
to the general flight of jets,
as they pretend to climb
over human weather, and land
on cement deserts that have
nothing to do with love.
I am overcast always
for having flown to escape
wild chicory I might
have picked for my wife, the man
next door I hate, and this
lousy city that managed,
without God, to smog itself
through another November day.
If I were pilot tomorrow,
I'd fly for better weather;
but tonight I'm not even
myself: where I haven't been
is already yesterday.

AFTER THE *THRESHER*

*a submarine
sunk with all hands
off the Atlantic shelf,
April 10, 1963*

There must be people, if
there are still people, who
somewhere yet above us

(where there are even birds)
breathe, swim, and survive
at their bright apogee

while we, under pressure,
gasp, weigh on each other,
and collapse face to face.

Even this sea-level smog
would seem like graced light
to signalmen tapping out code

from a locked hull, sounding
their own slow taps from the coast's
dark beer-can floor.

Trying to face them, we stretch
to imagine release, fail
to imagine ourselves, and try

to decompress with another
iced drink: the lawnspray squeaks,
and traffic begins to thunder

as if it were Sunday somewhere.
But we have been sunk for months,
under tons of possible air.

DEER ISLE

Out-island once, on a South slope
bare in March, I saw a buck
limp out of the spruce and snow
to ease his gut in a hummocky meadow.

He fed two rooted hours on the hope
of spring, browsed, and flicked back
into the trees, a big ghost
of what hunters tracked at first frost.

That was six winters ago. Today,
three hundred miles South, a commuter
trapped by a detour sign
at dusk, I trailed a reflecting line

of red arrows that took me the long way
home. Late, caught in the neuter
traffic, driven beyond where I wanted
to go, I braked by a slanted

orchard where six cars were stopped.
There were six does there, feeding on frozen
winesaps, fat and white-rumped
as the drivers who sat in their cars. One limped,

and I thought of that buck, equipped
to survive, on the island he'd chosen
to swim to. That coast, about now,
would lie gray: the raw salt snow

topping a man's hauled lobsterpots,
and sifting down through thick spruce

where the sweat on a run buck
would freeze. A man with no luck

but a gun would be hunting home cross-lots.
I was parked miles beyond choice,
miles from home on a blocked curve
in the dead midst of a thick suburban preserve.

My guts clamped. I honked my way clear,
tramping the gas toward nowhere
but where home was. My wife understood.
If I didn't go now, I never would.

TENANTS' HARBOR

Listen, the tide has turned:
you can hear yesterday's left-
over swell, fooling around

against Condon's Rock. Who's
to care where the cold front went,
when it lifted a week of nimbus

clear of the Camden Hills?
Somebody's probably mapped it,
as part of a spiral,

current from Canso
to Gander; people are always
pulsing their plot of distance

from storms, from a weapons-system,
a star, or a war. Safe
from radar, we're eased home

by how the wind climbed out
of the cove, and leaned Orion
down to this summer's last night.

Tomorrow, counting our change
at a tollgate, we'll suck
on a hot inland orange

for lunch, gas up to anchor
ourselves to a map, and plot
the cost of a winter ashore.

Tonight we only chart
ourselves, in how through spruce
the thick stars constellate.

This side of Condon's Rock
we're tenant to two black ducks,
discussing themselves in the dark.

Who's to tell them the world
lies elsewhere? Not you,
nor I, who migrate. The world

is wherever we quiet to hear it.
Tides darken our listening;
comic as ducks, we share it.

IV

CROSSTREES

He'd followed the telephone wires for miles, a wire
on each arm of the poles' tall crosstrees. Now
the ground was level, a kind of plateau.

Save for the poles and their solo wires high
on each crossarm, he'd been for two days above treeline.
The deer were small, their miniature faces facing

away from him as they browsed; they fed back over
the treeless distance he had already come.
Even at noon, the stunted deer sought

no cover; the last fawn he passed, at arm's length,
fed blind on white lichen. He couldn't
recall having climbed: the long horizon

behind him was flat in familiar sun, the marrow
of each hard crossarm sharply wired to
its own hard shadow. For two days now

he had not been afraid; but now, in his third dry dawn,
the sky would not quicken. He felt like a deer
gone blind in that morning's bright haze. But then

it opened: where wires from the nearest crossarm
sagged into infinite sunlight, out into what
might have once been across but was not,

the plateau split to a depth without bottom.
His eyes locked on the gap they met, he grabbed
for the ground with his knees and held on;

his eyes closed down to stretch focus. His wrists
pressed back at the edge, against the steep thrust
of a miniature city: a city so deeply sunk

that its buildings had no foundation, but
lifted clear in their own improbable light.
They were pockmarked with caves, but warm as the wall

in a painting of martyrs. Save for the wires
stretched over him, humming gently, thinned into
nowhere, nothing was filigree here: the beechtree

centered within the city bared its dead limbs
in brilliant cantilever; the sandtraps roofing
each building were perfectly raked, the tines

of each rake turned up and left naked.
He dug his toes into the hard plateau, trying
to trench his way back to known maps or

nameable wars. *Jesus God,* he said, before
the deer nosed toward him, *I once shot a thirty-two
on the back nine at Delft. And now I'm not even*

*myself, with nobody left to tell what I
came to, or how I got here or where it was.* The sun,
when he said these things, was still climbing, and

would not let him let go or draw back to sleep.
Jesus God, he said, when the time came. The mouths
of the deer were soft as the mouths of sheep.

TO CHEKHOV

in a November when I
could bear to read
nobody else

Finally
I have come to you.

Out from behind
hard mountains that looked

like the Urals when I
looked back a last time, back

across the low river,
the old rope-ferry sagging

downstream: I think, now,
of the ferryman weighed

by the army greatcoat
I left him on the far bank.

My gray mare dances sideways
across the shadowless steppe,

spooked by my hatless
shadow. Whenever we reach

the Donetz Station, where you
are already waiting, I have

to tell you how a fat
troika-driver, going the other

way, tipped me his hat,
and why I could not salute back.

And you, I expect, will know
his three geldings by name;

and will tell me the driver's
story, knowing who owns him,

and by what human motive,
on this particular

day, he drove his troika
to mountains beyond the river.

There is much about myself
that I do not believe;

much about the river,
and every mountain behind it,

I cannot yet love.
Yet owing to what you

wrote me, I ride to meet you.
Slowed as I am by how

my mind drifts sideways,
I give my mare free reign,

dancing sideways toward
the Donetz Station: you

will be there, waiting,
to tell me where I've been.

LINES FROM AN ORCHARD
ONCE SURVEYED BY THOREAU

I've lived by the world's rules
long enough. That season is over.
There's no ladder, no word that the bees
haven't already given. My feet
press cider back to the roots.
The orchard quiets; I sip
at its silence, letting the nectar
change me. What else
need I know, when there's
nothing to know, save
for the wisdom of trees?
I conduct myself like a naked monk.
Were I to open
to any more fullness, I think I'd
turn into a woman.

SUPPOSITION WITH QUALIFICATION

If he could say it, he meant to.
Not what it meant, if he ever knew,

but how it felt when he let himself
feel—even afraid of himself—

yet in that moment opened
himself to how the moment happened.

He meant to give himself up:
to how it could be when he gave up

requiring that each event shape
itself to his shape, his hope,

and intent. He meant not to weigh it,
whatever happened; only to let it

balance in its own light, to let light
fall where it would. If he could say it.

THANKSGIVING

The tides in my eye are heavy.
My grandmother's house wears oakleaves
instead of nasturtiums; hollyhocks
dry in the front-porch gutter.
I must have been a bad boy,
exiled under the attic stairs:
a hardwood hatrack plants
its Black-Eyed petals under my nose,
but I have no hat to top it.
I reach, instead, to touch the face
of the harvest moon, full on the face
of my mother's grandfather's clock.
My fingers tick, but the clock
will not relent; I cannot wind
nor strike it.
                    I only smell
the locked closets, the open shelves
of jarred preserves that grow
their quiet mold in the old back pantry.
My ears are mice, peaked to the sizzle
of badly bottled homemade rootbeer.
It was once Thanksgiving all week.
And we ate all day from the five pies
baked in the coalstove oven—after
the peas put up from summer, and squash
put down in the cellar. I cannot say
what else lies under my tongue.
My mother's mouth is grave with snow;
on the hill where she, too, was once young.

HARD COUNTRY

In hard
country each white
house, separated
by granite outcrop
from each white
house, pitches
its roofline
against the hard sky.
Hand-split
shakes, fillet
and face plank, clap-
board, flashing
and lintel: every
fit part over-
laps from the ridge
board on down, wind-
tight and water-
tight, down
to the sideyard back
door, shut against
eavesdrop.

Nobody
takes storm windows
off: each blank
pane, framed by
its own sharp
molding, looks out
without shutters at
juniper, granite,
and hackmatack.

Granite takes
nothing for granted,
hackmatack's spiny;
junipers mind their
ledged roots. Save
for a day when its back
door opens on lilac,
there isn't a house
in this country
that sleeps or
wakes

In hard
country Orion,
come summer, hunts
late; but belts its
prime stars all
winter when sun
is short: each white
house, separated
by granite outcrop
from each white
house, pitches
its private roof
against horizon
and season; each white
clapboard, wind-
tight and water-
tight, juts
against weather
its own four inches
of shadow and
light.

LABRADOR RIVER

A half-day North of Nain,
on the South bank of the Fraser River,

two men sit hunched in blown snow.
One wears a hat like a red wool mitten.

He's wrapped in fur; the other is hooded in
a hide anorak. Slightly apart,

but married to their decision, a woman
in a white parka waits with them, her back

turned to the river they face. A fourth figure,
nearest the river, is insulated from all

the rest; he might be only
a slumped stone cairn. Three, then,

or four: the wind behind them has blown
stiff clumps of grass bare, and peaked

the hood of the woman's white parka.
The Fraser is frozen solid, its salt ice

waved by sastrugi; on the river's
far bank, beyond stunted conifers,

the smoked horizon is long without sun.
No boat is due this season; they don't

expect the boat. Native, they know
they're halfway to the Pole; they don't need stars

to remind them of that. Nor do they
want maps or charts of this coast;

they have every inlet by heart. Why
or how they got here, nobody's said.

Maybe somebody left a question
hanging; or maybe, this half-day North

of Nain, on the South bank of the Fraser,
there's an answer they've barely got wind of.

The wind in its own right searches their wrists.
Hunched against it, expectantly dressed,

the three (or four) of them hold their meeting.
They are met. They hold. They are waiting.

V

ENTRY

Sheer cold here.
Four straight days
below zero, the roof
contracting in
small explosions
all night. Now snow:
snow halfway up
the back shed;
more coming all
morning: the sky
drifted, patched
blue, flakes in
large sizes
lazing against
a small sun.
Around here
they call
these days "open
and shut," by
sunset the wind
will veer and
stiffen; tomorrow
will build on
a windblown
crust. Given
this day, none
better, I try
these words to
quicken
the silence: I
break track
across it
to make myself
known.

STOVE

I wake up in the bed my grandmother died in.
November rain. The whole house is cold.
Long stairs, two rooms through to the kitchen:
walls that haven't been painted
in sixty years. They must have shone then:
pale sun, new pumpkin, old pine.

Nothing shines now but the nickel trim
on the grandmother stove, an iron invention
the whole room leans to surround; even
when it is dead the dogs sleep close behind it.
Now they bark out, but let rain return them;
they can smell how the stove is going to be lit.

Small chips of pine from the woodshed. Then
hardwood kindling. I build it all into the firebox,
on top of loose wads of last June's *Bangor News*.
Under the grate, my first match
catches. Flames congregate, the dogs watch,
the stove begins to attend old wisdom.

After the first noisy moments, I listen for Lora;
she cooked all the mornings my grandmother died,
she ruled the whole kitchen the year I was seven:
I can see Boyd Varnum, a post outside the side door;
he's waiting for Lora, up in the front of the house,
to get right change for his winter squash. Lora says

Boyd's got the best winter squash in the village.
When Boyd gets paid, she ties her apron back on
and lets in the eggman. He has a green wagon.

Lora tells him how last night her husband hit her;
she shows him the marks. All her bruised arms
adjust dampers and vents; under the plates where turnips

are coming to boil, she shifts both pies in the oven.
The dogs feel warmer now. I bank on thick coal.
The panes steam up as sure as November: rain,
school, a talkative stove to come home to at noon;
and Lora sets my red mittens to dry on the nickel shelves
next to the stovepipe. Lora knitted my mittens.

I can still smell the litter of spaniels
whelped between the stove and the wall; there's
venison cooking, there's milktoast being warmed on
the furthest back plate, milktoast to send upstairs
to my dead mother's mother. Because, Lora says,
she is sick. Lora says she is awful sick. When Lora goes up

to my grandmother's bed, I play with the puppies
under the stove; after they suckle and go back to sleep,
because I am in second grade and am seven, I practice
reading the black iron letters raised on the black oven door;
even though I don't know who Queen Clarion was,
I'm proud I can read what the oven door says: it says

> *Queen Clarion*
> *Wood & Bishop*
> *Bangor, Maine*
> *1911*

63

A LATE SPRING: EASTPORT

On the far side
of the storm
window, as close

as a tree
might grow to
a house,

beads of rain
hang cold
on the lilac:

at the tip of
each twig each
bud swells green;

tonight out
there each
branch will be

glazed, each
drop will
freeze solid:

the ice, at
sunrise, will
magnify every

single
bud; by this
time next

week, in-
side this
old glass,

the whole
room will
bloom.

THE WAY TIDE COMES

It came close from out far,
the way tide comes, changing
its levels with such consistent
slowness that—before I
knew it—height became depth,
and where you danced barefoot,

a half tide ago, covered itself,
under so moving a shimmer
I could not conceive of the weight,
or recall all those shapes
the weight, as it climbed, erased.
We'd kept to old ways, building

a beachfire well above tideline,
ritual at the pure height of summer;
we'd piled driftwood on,
all we could gather. I was
skipping flat stones, you
were trying to keep count; leaning

to throw, I felt distances shift:
it was no longer coming but
like the light of summer itself,
longest the day when summer began,
had already flooded and made
its insistent turn. As once it came

slowly, so now it pulls back
with the quick of evening light:
it will, in due time, uncover

the furthest rocks we swam up on,
even the morning shallows where we
first waded. Tonight's full moon

has already cast off the horizon
it hugely climbed; it's going, before
long, to tug the whole cove empty.
We slept once pretending a larger
knowledge; now we love better.
Let love be; let the heel-and-toe

of your improvised jig, marginal
even at noon, or my sweater,
speared by the branch of a beachlog,
remain our private highwater mark.
There's nothing left, nothing to add,
for which the tide will not account:

fire, our awkward toes where
we yield, the periwinkles' slow track;
no matter how we want, beyond doubt,
to stay the tide or inform it, we
come in time to inform ourselves: we have
to follow it all the way out.

ADDING IT UP

My mind's eye opens before
the light gets up. I
lie awake in the small dark,
figuring payments, or how
to scrape paint; I count
rich women I didn't marry.
I measure bicycle miles
I pedaled last Thursday
to take off weight; I give some
passing thought to the point
that if I hadn't turned poet
I might well be some other
sort of accountant. Before
the sun reports its own weather
my mind is openly at it:
I chart my annual rainfall,
or how I'll plant seed if
I live to be fifty. I look up
words like "bilateral symmetry"
in my mind's dictionary; I consider
the bivalve mollusc, re-pick
last summer's mussels on Condon Point,
preview the next red tide, and
hold my breath: I listen hard
to how my heart valves are doing.
I try not to get going
too early: bladder permitting,
I mean to stay in bed until six;
I think in spirals, building
horizon pyramids, yielding to
no man's flag but my own.

I think a lot of Saul Steinberg:
I play touch football on one leg,
I seesaw on the old cliff, trying
to balance things out: job,
wife, children, myself.
My mind's eye opens before
my body is ready for its
first duty: cleaning up after
an old-maid Basset in heat.
That, too, I inventory:
the Puritan strain will out,
even at six a.m.; sun or no sun,
I'm Puritan to the bone, down to
the marrow and then some:
if I'm not sorry I worry,
if I can't worry I count.

WEAR

I hate how things wear out.

Not elbows, collars, cuffs;
they fit me, lightly frayed.

Not belts or paint or rust,
not routine maintenance.

On my own hook I cope
with surfaces: with all

that rubs away, flakes off, or fades
on schedule. What eats at me

is what wears from the in-
side out: bearings, couplings,

universal joints, old
differentials, rings,

and points: frictions hidden
in such dark they build

to heat before they come
to light. What gets to me

is how valves wear, the slow
leak in old circuitry,

the hairline fracture under
stress. With all my heart

I hate pumps losing prime,
immeasurable over-

loads, ungauged fatigue
in linkages. I hate

myself for wasting time
on hate: the cost of speed

came with the bill of sale,
the rest was never under

warranty. Five years
ago I turned in every

year; this year I rebuild
rebuilt parts. What hurts

is how blind tired I get.

DREAMSCAPE

On the steep road
curving to town, up
through spruce trees
from the filled-in canal,
there have been five houses, always.

But when I sleep
the whole left side of the blacktop
clears itself into good pasture.
There are two old horses,
tethered. And a curving row
of miniature bison, kneeling,

each with his two front hooves
tucked in neatly under the lip
of the asphalt. I am asleep.
I cannot explain it. I do not
want to explain it.

A DREAM OF RUSSIA

On the Trans-Siberian
Railroad, far
East of the Urals, years
before the last war,
the Eastbound train
cranked to a stop
in the absolute
middle of nowhere.

We all got out.

It was high summer,
it must have been June,
in that labored cut
through the low
hills, somewhere
west of Omsk; the fields
were full of buttercups.

A conductor, tipping
his cap, came up to tell us
the last car had a hotbox;
the axle of the last truck
was, for a fact, burnt out.
It would take an hour to fix,
perhaps two hours.

The men smoked.
They stood at ease on
the roadbed; the women
climbed up the bank
into pastures.

Somebody in authority
must have telegraphed
ahead, perhaps
to Omsk, or back
to someone he knew
in Moscow.

The men walked back
alongside the track
as they smoked, to inspect
the burnt-out truck.
It had melted all right, the cap-
end of the axle, melted
beyond repair.

We waited under that empty
Russian sky for more
than an hour, while
the hotbox end of the axle
cooled from red hot
to lukewarm. Men spat on it,
or patted it, to tell;
they made bets. But nobody
seemed to doubt that help
would eventually come.

It came, all right! Oh it
came: a blur
becoming four men, rolling
in front of them—up
the long track behind us—
a widening great steel axle,
a new axle and two new wheels, welded
as one.

While we cheered them on,
and the trainwhistle blew
from the engine end, the women
returned to the top of the cut,
standing with hiked-up skirts against
the near horizon,
humming some Russian song.

Then the conductor
directed the men,
perhaps a hundred men,
to lift
the last car.

They heaved and did it,
swearing a great
conglomerate oath,
as though they were moving
heaven and earth.

He held them there for
the crucial minute,
conducting in that same dialect
he must have sent
by telegraph. And while
they held, new men
moved out the old axle;
and those four men
from somewhere back toward the Urals
rolled in the new one. Then
the conductor gave
a signal; they let down easy, and
there she was.

All this was years
before the last war, somewhere
east of the Urals.
I tell you that trainwhistle blew
while the men climbed back aboard
and we got ready to start toward
the east again
on the Trans-Siberian
Railroad: East toward
Omsk and Lake Chany and,
in another week,
Vladivostok.

It had taken exactly two hours.

Oh, when that whistle blew
the women came down from
the railroad bank
and the long pastures
behind them; they pelted
the axle-pushers with skirts full
of buttercups, of what looked like
daisies, and with wild hundreds
and hundreds of wild Russian
flowers.

HOW TO SEE DEER

Forget roadside crossings.
Go nowhere with guns.
Go elsewhere your own way,

lonely and wanting. Or
stay and be early:
next to deep woods

inhabit old orchards.
All clearings promise.
Sunrise is good,

and fog before sun.
Expect nothing always;
find your luck slowly.

Wait out the windfall.
Take your good time
to learn to read ferns;

make like a turtle:
downhill toward slow water.
Instructed by heron,

drink the pure silence.
Be compassed by wind.
If you quiver like aspen

trust your quick nature:
let your ear teach you
which way to listen.

You've come to assume
protective color; now
colors reform to

new shapes in your eye.
You've learned by now
to wait without waiting;

as if it were dusk
look into light falling:
in deep relief

things even out. Be
careless of nothing. See
what you see.

THE INCREDIBLE YACHTS

The incredible yachts: stays
and halyards geared to tension,
banks of winches on deck;
they blew into harbor
this evening: richly cruised men
wed to aluminum hulls
and fleet women: they raced
to get here. Once at anchor
in this stormed harbor,
in this indelible weather,
they bobbled the tide with
their empties: none of them
cared to know in truth
what harbor they were in.

PRIDES CROSSING

Born to Prides Crossing,
privately tutored; finished

at Foxcroft, engaged to
Groton and Harvard, wed

after the Coral Sea
and Midway; bride

to Treasury, wife
to Wall Street and mother

to Gracie Square, she
has been first mate

on three Bermuda races,
and is newly mistress

of one round-the-world
teak ketch. Aboard,

at her grandfather's
inlaid desk, far in

the Caribbean, she
times to her forty-

sixth birthday
her annual letter

to her last tutor.
Her hand is impeccably

North Shore italic:
Since Arthur's corporate

interests require him
to be in Aruba one day

and North of the Arctic
Circle the next, we

live somewhat separate
lives. Whit has been

asked to depart St. Paul's,
after drugs; we don't know

where he goes next. Jilly,
whom you last saw

the summer she was about
to start Chapin,

I have just now flown back
to New York to abort.

I have been hospitalized
myself, but am out

again for a third try.
At least I refuse

what my friends still
in Boston seem nowadays

to feast on: the sacrilege
of an easy Jesus.

Please do not
send me condolences;

I know you will not.
Her script slants

increasingly small: *I sit*
to write you aboard

an anchored sailboat, with my
own name on her transom.

She is perfectly furled. I
am afloat, the crew is ashore;

every halyard and sheet
is perfectly coiled. I sit

wondering, now, if life
will ever unbraid

itself. Or do
I mean unsnarl

itself? I know that you
cannot tell me this. . . .

But how, if it does,
will I know that it has?

IT IS BEING

It is being offshore: nothing that's not horizon.
It is, beyond beacons, sailing alone.
Nothing, beyond one's compass, to point or warn.

It is, as necessity, knowing the old names for stars
blanked by cloud. To home on them is,
as it's given, to steer a singular course:

it is to navigate knowing that no port is home.
It is to assign one's self to the helm;
it is, offshore, repeating for sanity one's own name,

on watch beyond relief. It is standing watch
beyond hope of relief, weathering the blind fetch
of one's heart, and the crabbed set of one's mind.

It is tacking in fog. It is, of a stillness,
to fish with deep hooks. And, if they catch, to bless
with strange names from the masthead all you release.

Where there is nothing that's not horizon
it is, to ease thirst, sucking a fishbone.
It is being outside one's limits, the horizon's one man.

WAYS

Gratefully,
with family around;
held to known hands:
the old way.
*

In a motel bathroom,
unable to get to
the phone.
*

While sirens flash,
watching blood channel;
trapped in the bite
of acetylene torches.
*

Fog and a mountain:
the warning lights pulse.
A belt in the gut.
All of you.
*

Feeling for handholds
on a sheer face,
cheek to cold stone.
*

The pain,
weighing tons,
shifting.
*

In prison,
the end of a sentence.
*

A red flannel shirt,
jogging, against
traffic.

*
Running uphill
through old films,
under orders.
                *
Hearing the whistle
that notes
a trajectory.
                *
Tubes at both ends;
paying for it.
Not even the nurses
can smile.
                *
Cells eating cells:
childish arithmetic
followed by zeros.
Strangers: counting.
Relatives: counting.
Strangers and relatives,
counting. And counting.
                *
Drunk, a half hour before sunrise.
Unable, for once, not
to reach for the gun.
                *
Still listening for music.
A band at the corner:
turning maybe this way.
Or that.
                *
Barely come out
of your doctor's brick office:

counting, already,
how friends will figure.

Figuring, newly,
the ways old friends managed.

Managing courage:
weeks of more tests.

WORD

In a flat month
in a low field

I hit on a word
with just one

meaning. One.
It got to me,

hard. I stood
back up, grabbing

for balance; I
tried to hit

back. But it
meant it: no

matter what I
did nothing

would yield.
I tried old

levers: hope,
belief, love.

Earth would not
give, not for

the world. Not
one prospect

of any appeal.
That was final:

the world itself
would have the last

word; no way
around it, over,

or through. No
reason behind it.

Who, in God's name,
had what in mind?

I dug as deep as
my heart could stand.

NATURAL HISTORY

March: a porcupine spent
March nights gnawing sap
from the blue spruce trunk;

he climbed two-thirds of
the cold March branches
before he bit into the bark.

A tree as tall as a house.
Now, midsummer, the sprucegum
still bleeds; like a root

cut quick by the blade
of a mower, the whole upper trunk
slowly gums up.

The porcupine trespasses
still, waddling toward evening
across the backyard like

a dirty quilled panda.
The two dogs might smile,
if they could. They hold back,

from experience. The porcupine,
fat as a garbage pail,
admits, to his nocturnal

seasons, no moral.
The spruce, through July,
dies without sorrow.

GRAFFITO

My father, 79,
died in his home bed
with no last word,
his jawbone frozen open.

Before the service
while the chimes said
nothing, I—afraid I
might die the same way—

ran to a men's room
deep in the chapel.
Letting go, I read
pencil on marble:

Time is nature's way
of preventing
everything
from happening all at once.

Father, forgive
my unforgiving mouth:
I sang how those words sang,
I felt the whole stall dance.

STRIP

Möbius knew: he
figured it out:

this complex plane
does not, by

any equation,
add up to

zero.
It happens barely:

after the turn,
opposites start

to connect,
the event

becomes an act
of relief:

a continuous
map of how, in

half-turning,
a man

can surface to
change; he thumbs

his way home
the long way

around, from
where he is

to where he
intends: he

finds himself
turning

back into
himself.

LIVES

I

A far coast.
The dark come down early.
Down over the hill, the harbor.
The old heaved sidewalk. By nine
not even a houselight still on.

Under the one corner streetlight
two new figures: they stand strange.
And now another. No car, out of nowhere.
Then here, this corner.

We talk.
        Strange
so familiar: after
a funeral in Halifax once.
It's true. I even imagine
I know the third one.

The draggers start bunting the spiles,
the tide must have turned.

We go down in the dark to see.

Against the pull of the ebb
there are fish who sound small,
flipping the surface.
                Fish
after fish.
        We listen,
watching the dark.

As if it weren't winter
we swing legs over
the edge of the wharf.

The scallop season opens
at midnight, the men already collecting
under the single light.

What a life.

We haul each other back up.

II
What a life.

Seasons of leaves, interstices
of pure light. Holy days:
solstice and equinox; cold
coming clear and tipping
the balance. We grow
to be old.

The store, the mail, stopping
for gas; mornings of evening
invitations.
       Everyone lives
as though no one knew.

III
Driven home late:
         same old Chevy, same
kid-argument.
        High on headlights, a deer
settles it: sprung almost across the road
in one leap.

Almost.
                    The curve,
the centrifugal pull of a sixpack.
                    The power line arcs.
All down the line
all the lights
go out.
                    Or a dog, the next noon,
                    in a first spit
of snow. He goes
for the joy of it, running
the wind.   Then, when it
stops, the wind of quick cars. Car
after car.
            Then a gull,
headed crosswind.
                    The driver gets out
and walks back.
                    The blood of the world
floods the dog's mouth.
                        People who know better
cruise after church,
                    spotting the sites;
close to bared apples, they stop
by the Grange where deer browse.
                            Four days to wait,
                            a short season
this year: headlights at dusk
flick down the woods-roads. Guns
racked against the backwindow
of pickups.
                Back in the store
the men talk of bearscat.

IV

His wife and son left, a boy
in a loft far inland sleeping off
grief.
              Mice. Winter squash.

He gets up in the cold to do *t'ai chi*.
The first time since July.
Everything in him quivers.

I am learning to be quiet, to listen,
to balance, to try for the balance of us all
whether to continue or to cease.

Behind him the wind clear-cuts the hillside.

Leaves at his feet, the ground frozen,
he stretches, feels his muscles remember each other,
balances, holds, and eases.

I ask myself now as I look at these I's
if there is something to be said
past the realization that there is nothing
to be said.

Parsnips, turnips, hard squash, the root
shapes. A whole spring catalogue
come to bear on the floor of the loft.
They weigh, grown to nightmare.

It is cold in the loft, and when
I do sleep it is sound.

Beyond sleep, in the hardwood valley
where deer in their season
will finally come down,

a hundred Presidents hang racked
on a single tree, each
like a small boy's school-window moon.

I think of the places
we loved. The shore, tides,
the years.
                    Moved, they've
gone far. Moved, the boy
writes his letter

much love
                    and walks all the way
into Conway to mail it.
                    Miles
of valley carved by the river,
whole geologic ages.
                    Old foothills.
He feels them close:
                    millions
of rains on the ridges.

V
The first hard freeze, three calm nights without let-up.
This third morning, black ice:
                         the surface
flowered with frost, the whole marsh frozen into
a stillness:
                    the windless channels give way
to islands of marshgrass, bleached ninetails;
                                   the reaches
edge behind larch to maple; beyond their silver,
whole horizons of fir.
                    We sit on mittens,
lacing old skates.

                    I watch you happen to smile,
wondering how we ever came
                       to love.
Next to the outlet, a big pipe under a country road,
the black ice skims to nothing;
                             wondering where
the source is, we skate a surface
                           barely safe:
the new ice sinks and swells as it takes up
our weight;
               reports crack ahead of us,
blazing our passage, mapping it.
                             We skate to a drum
we half create, run out of wind
                    and stop, still.
The sky's brittle.
                    Airbubbles pumped out of nowhere
freeze under our feet in mid-ice:
                         schools of loosed stars,
small planets,
             and moons come to nought.
Surveyors of space
                new to us, we focus down
through galaxies
             to eelgrass waving in soft currents;
beetles small as a dot
              swim at large under
the planets.

We slide a foot toward what an old man wrote
the week before he died:
we live, we have
             to live, on
                 insufficient
evidence.

It's true: brightly stilted, surfaced on dense shallows,
we steady each other by
                    studying a slow green dance:
newts and frogs
                    tunneled into the silt,
maybe with crayfish and perch
                              covered by last summer's layers:
planaria, husks of dragonflies.
                              Through the ice,
darkly, we half see
                    how the heron lives; frozen out,
the ducks and he
                    took off for God knows where.
The chickadee in the hackmatack whistles his calling across
the marsh, a small solace
                         where we skate
                                   filled
with an absence.
                  Who knows what we did to help? Who
                  knows, ever, how to give what's due?
It's true:
          we never know
               a life
                    enough. . . .

The black ice cracks and holds:
you pump off hard
to the beaver house
                    your far eye just discovered.

Now you shout back
                    through first thin snow
what only the beaver
can hear, or only
the pickerel and hornpout

                    nosed into mud,
or the painted turtle we'll come back to count
                                    next spring.
Close to the source
                    I ease across flexible ice
to catch you:
                opening ourselves
                between ninetails and snow
                        we come close
                                    and hug:
                                        lives
we barely know, lives
                    we keep wanting
to know.

VI

NOT TO TELL LIES

He has come to a certain age.
To a tall house older than he is.
Older, by far, than he ever will be.
He has moved his things upstairs, to a room
which corners late sun. It warms a schooner model,
his daughter's portrait, the rock his doctor brought him
back from Amchitka. When he looks at the rock he thinks Melville;
when he touches the lichen he dreams Thoreau. Their testaments
shelve the inboard edge of the oak-legged table he writes on.
He has nailed an ancestor's photograph high over his head.
He has moored his bed perpendicular to the North wall;
whenever he rests his head is compassed barely west
of Polaris. He believes in powers: gravity, true
North, magnetic North, love. In how his wife
loved the year of their firstborn. When-
ever he wakes he sees the clean page in
his portable. He has sorted life out;
he feels moved to say all of it,
most of it all. He tries
to come close, he keeps
coming close: he has
gathered himself
in order not
to tell
lies.

▲

Aside from the life
I live inside it,
this room is nothing.
Nothing invades it.
I try to figure: I
am more vital than it;
that is my virtue: not
in my own life to live
as if nothing
were more important.

▼

WORDS FOR THE ROOM

Today's a long season after Thanksgiving.
I got up early, let out the dogs, and ate.
I've got almost four almost-right poems,

and one quick typewriter set before me,
plus a silvery Piels Real Draft, already
half empty at my left hand. I sit

on the right hand of Saint Jarrell, despairing,
trying to mind an old heart that is, in spite
of itself, almost full. I love my children,

I'm stunned by my grandson, renewed by my wife.
I almost have poems. And, to complete them,
hundreds of words, a whole dark roomful to choose from.

Words for the room: a new ceiling, a door.
That's all, they're all, between me and the world;
nothing but choice, nothing save will:

infinitives, relative objects. I can feel,
I can name, what I have to decide: I mean
if I mean to revise my whole life.

▲

In this gray depression
I try to sleep off, or
wake from, nothing connects.
Nothing gets to me. In that
there is nothing to say,
I have to begin with nothing.
In that there is nothing
to feel, there's nothing
I'd better question. I find
myself far into mid-life
willing at last to begin.

▼

FALLING APART

The windows stay.
The clapboards go wavy.
The high branches look
to belong to the elm.

It's inside things
don't arrive right: how
far from my good eye
this left fist is; or
this swelled thumb. How long
my neck has refused to
hold up its head. Parts
of me disincline; I lean
in a lot of directions,
all without compass.

There isn't fog, but
it's gray all day: gray
in the elms' old elbows,
gray in my bowels. Cracks
in the clapboard want paint.
My hand thinks my head
needs more room on the sill.
There are holes where some-
body took out the nails.

Only the windows stay.

FLINCHING

Crossing from where he has been
to where he even less wants to go,

hollow of sleep, faced by the moon,
he feels animals in him eat at their reins.

Marooned between lines of opposing traffic,
he tries to get off the island ledge:

he prays to Kochab, and wakes without sun,
the morning opera already howling.

Distrusting the natives two valleys west,
he steals along clamflats; waves

breed waves twice as high as his head:
wherever he moves is over the edge.

▲

Noam was in intensive care when he came to.
The truck hit the taxi, the taxi jumped the curb,
sideswiped him and felled his wife, then twisted
back at him.

            Heigh-ho, the dairy-o,
she'd just gone out to buy milk . . .

Noam saw the replay before the nurse came on:
Don't worry, *she said,* you're going
to be all right. Nothing
is going to happen.
I know, *Noam said,* it already has.

▼

OF WHALES AND MEN: 1864

The possible
world:
      a man
named Svend Foyn

invented
the end:
        we began
to explode
inside:
        what struck us
stuck:
      we died,
slowly,
of the barb

charged
to tow us:
        it came
in time
to be general

practice.

A SLOW BREAKER

Washing on granite
before it turns
on itself, away

from every horizon
it fetched from,
this clear green wash,

the flashing, cold,
specific gravity of it,
calls the eye down

to what we thought to
look into, to all we
cannot see through.

RECALL

Father,
　　　Without you, I drift off at work
with a dream you must have slept with
for years:
　　　　　that spanking-new '34 Chevy
parked at the top of the steep cement ramp
in the brick garage where you always bought cars
in the town I could never grow up in.

I went with you the day they delivered:
the cream wheels, the plush smell, the braided cord for
a laprobe—a car I've had stored so long
I forgot it.
　　　　　I barely wake now,
cold Aprils after your dying, to this green car
mother paid for, this dream I've slept on
for hundreds of seasons, this face in the rear-view mirror
that looks more like yours
than my own;
　　　　　I own to it now:
the way I have to reclaim what I've left,
the way I need to get myself back.

▲

His nurse, at bedside, said What is it?
Nothing, *Noam said,* it's nothing.

He heard her keep saying I want to know.
No, *he said,* nobody wants to.

I tell you I do. I want
to know. Where does it hurt?

It doesn't, it's
nothing, nothing at all.

You're trying to cry, it's got
to be hurting.

I tell you it's nothing,
nothing is all.

▼

FOG

Winded, drifting to rest,
                    I'm rowing
between islands, between pewter water
and a gauze I'm unwinding that winds back
behind me in my flat wake.
                              At the tip
of each oar small vortices whorl
at each stroke's end.
                    If I looked down through
I could see Stephen who swam for his friend
on his eighth birthday. Or Mr. Ames,
swept overboard at daybreak, racing
big seas off Greenland. Or his boys
who went after him.
                    They were my heroes
the June I was nine. It's different now:
with no horizon, with the end
of the century coming up,
                    I'm rowing
where measure is lost, I'm barely moving,
in a circle of translucence that moves with me
without compass.
                    I can't see out or up into;
I sit facing backwards,
                        pulling myself slowly
toward the life I'm still trying to get at.

▲

Nothing is sure.
Nothing in me
approaches nothing
constantly; though
I approach nothing
at a constant rate,
the process, as
we close, seems
to accelerate.

▼

RATES

A caterpillar, long
beyond summer, crossing
the blacktop
east of Machias

  Copernicus Leonardo Luther

a fingerling headed
downstream, in
an eddy

  Galileo Shakespeare Newton

pinwheeling out in
M-101, a white dwarf dead
before history was born

  Bach Voltaire Diderot Hume

the black mark spun
through the meter downcellar,
a bulb left on in the attic
all winter

  Kant Mozart Blake

forsythia, barely
unfolded, out on
the outskirts
of Gander

  Darwin Marx Van Gogh

a tern, its beak
quick with herring,
flying up through current to
sun

Freud   Picasso   Einstein

a far gun: while
smoke announces
something has started, air
withholding
its tall report.

GENERATION

A bald fifty-some,
                    shaving in
his dead father's
nickel-plated
                    extensible mirror
(patented 1902),
the father, stripped
                    to bathe, notes
his bare grandson
studying again, from
                    four-year-old
eye-level, the old
primary stem,
                    hanging out
from the apple-
pouch where he
                    remembers his father's,
presiding over
a wad of wirehair.
                    He shaves considering
all the trouble.

THE YOUNG

They keep doing it.
                Missing
the curve.
         Three, already,
in just this one year.
                The same
stretch, three different lives.

A telephone pole, a tree,
a stonewall
            The headlights hit
before the car rolls.
                They keep
doing it.
         Too much or too little,
in wrong combinations, too late.
Or too early.
                They keep missing
the curve.
           The siren.
                And in
a dark house the darkness through
hundreds of nights after the phone
begins its blind ring.

▲

We used to say Nothing's
too good for our kids.

Now we don't know what to say.

*Nothing seems to be good enough
for them. If everything isn't
just right, nothing will do.*

▼

DRAGGING

A whole week. Out of
the North all day.

A dry cold. The wind
clean as split oak.

Dark islands, dark as
the march of whitecaps.

Under hills hard on
the shoreline: churches,

settlements, planted
like bones. Out here,

the boat on good marks,
we let the wire out:

the drag plunges and
tugs. First light to

first dark, we tow, dump,
set, tow. Numb to what

cuts our hands, we set,
tow, dump, mend; tow until

dark closes down. We clean
the catch heading in

through dark to the thin
walls of our lives, grown

numb to the wind, numb
to the dark, to all we've

dragged for and taken,
shells returned to

that other dark that
weighs the whole bottom.

▲

Durward: setting his trawl
for haddock, and handlining cod
a half-mile East of Seal Island,

twelve miles offshore in fog.
Then his new engine went out.
A Rockland dragger spotted him,

two days later, drifting drunk
off Mount Desert Rock. He was
down to his last sixpack.

After they towed him back in,
Ordway kept asking him what
—those two days—he'd been thinking.

Nothin. I thought about nothin.
That was all there was to it.
Ord said, Y'must've thought something.

Nope, I thought about nothin.
You know what I thought,
I thought fuckit.

▼

POEM FOR THE TURN OF THE CENTURY

Wars ago, wars ago
                this dawn,
the sun come up under cloud,
up and into,
                men waded ashore
on some June beach
to die.
        At war again
with ourselves
at the century's turn
             again
we've set sail:
the shore we keep closing on
                comes clear
through the glass:
on the edge of a village
                steeped with windmills
people appear
to hill their crop
            with no weapon
beyond a hoe.
In the sinking distance
              we hailed from,
miles aft,
as the sun
          comes over
the cloudbank,
light takes
          the residual islands
like a wreath
laid on the sea.

▲

When the nurse finally brought in his bedpan,
Noam felt as certain as Luther of wisdom:

Diarrhea spelled backwards, *he told her,*
is, practically, air raid.

Whadidyasay? *she said.* Nothing,
Noam said, I said nothing.

▼

CALENDAR

Two months after
the birth of her
June child, she found

in her neighbor's
backyard that she
couldn't talk. She

ran inside to
write on a pad
don't worry, and

found she couldn't
write. New Year's night
she'd found a mole

grown wild on her
arm. Too many
lifetimes after

her neighbor held
her, her brother-
in-law came for

the child. She
shouted him out
the backdoor: *Look*

at me, I'm a
corpse. . . . He ran.
She came that close.

▲

The dark comes down
in white rooms where it
settles nothing.

The dead go on their own way

▼

OSSIPEE: NOVEMBER

The dark fold of the land:
steeped hills settling
a pond between them.

Black ice on the pond.
Glacial boulders in brooks
holding snow. Halfway up

the horizon, snowsqualls
tall against sun. A tree points,
spare on the clearcut spine

of a mountain. Wherever
it was the lightplane went down
won't unlock until April.

▲

Ord kept asking:
How'd it happen?
How'd he do it?

Everyone said
nobody knew.

Durward said,
Noam used to say
he'd been some
to a shrink . . .

Jesus, *Ordway*
said, he was
a shrink. You got
to go to one
to be one. It's
like signing-on
with a church.

All's I know,
Durward said,
Noam must've been
some good doctor.
He had himself
a built-in
shit detector.

Finest kind, *Ord said.*
But maybe that's what
clogged him up. Maybe

he couldn't stand
all he knew. Maybe he
didn't have any way
left to feel. A man
sits all day
on the edge of nothing,
after a while he
gets numb and falls in.

▼

SYNTAX

Short of words in that quick dark
where there was nothing between them,

he longed, in her, for some light verb
which, if she could, would ease him.

▲

Nothing is given.
Nothing is unforgiving.

▼

OLD MAN

This is a dream I needed.

I wake in my own old room
toward morning, lying next to the knees
of a girl—a young mother—born
in the milltown miles upriver.
Kneeling beside me, smiling,
she lets her long hair shelter me from
every view of myself. Except, out the dormer window,
the town's last elm.

I adore you
I tell her.
I know, she says,
with you I am quiet.

This is a sleep I am lucky to wake from.

By the time I walk down over the hill
for the *News*, she is opening her store.
She turns in the doorway, her son in arms,
and smiles. I nod and smile, trusting myself
not to say I adore her, trusting her
to dream what I have not said.

▲

No matter how I feel,
I am of several minds.

Nothing I think is as sure
as my mind's several voices.

▼

MARY'S, AFTER DINNER

Both hands talking, raised to shoulder height,
the left uptilted with a Lucky Strike,
the right still doubled down, inside of smoke,
across an opposite heart:
>   *the argument is nothing,*
nothing after all . . .
>   . . . all August that we've drunk,
made talk of, dined on, drawn back from,
then come back to sip;
>   the evening settled,
dearly, in your hands, the room
moves to the logic of your smile:
sitting full-face, unsurrender'd,
you say whole strophes from *Anon.,*
the truest poet of all;
>   more telling
than we knew, their measure
opens us to speak:
>   before the fire
your calendar has lit, brilliant
for the moment, we let words raise us
by their power:
>   we hear
our language validate our lives.

THINKING ABOUT HANNAH ARENDT

(1906–1975)

The kitchen stove wood-ash
I took out this morning,
to dress the snowfield
that covers the garden.

The ashwood I've blazed
to fell before dark:
a whole grove to go,
to limb and twitch out,
to yard and fit; then,
after all, let season.

This present fire.
This kitchen oven.

The cigarette smoke you inhaled, held deep,
and let drift, displaced
in Maine, telling
your fear in being a Jew
landing alone in
Damascus. At home
with how slowly
iron heats, with
how strange to
myself I am, I sit
by a stove as dark as
the mourning you wore
against snow. I lean
to the exquisite warmth
of your sadness, your
intricate face:
                your eyes clear
with a reason dear beyond reason.

THIS DAY AFTER YESTERDAY
Robert Trail Spence Lowell (1917–1977)

I
This day after yesterday.

Morning rain small on the harbor,
nothing that's not gray.

I heard at Hooper's, taking the Plymouth in
for brakes. Out from behind
his rolltop desk, Ken said, "*Ra*dio says
a *co*lleague of yours died. Yessir,
*died. Low*ell. Wasn't he your friend?"

Yesterday blazed, the Bay full of spindrift and sun.
If you'd looked down from your Ireland plane
I could have shared you twelve seals upriver,
seven heron in Warm Cove, and
an early evening meteor.
                    If I'd said such portents,
you would have flattened me with prepschool repartee,
your eyes owl'd out:
                    "And a poet up a fir tree . . ."

II
That's how friendship went.

At least this summer,

this last summer:
                    home,
almost home.

Ulysses come up over the beachstones,
shuffling with terrible age. We hugged and
parted, up the picnic field,
lugging tens of summers.

III
You wanted women, mail, praise.
What men thought of what you'd conquered.
Beyond the irony of fame, the honor due
to how a poet suffers: the brilliance of first drafts,
the strophe tinker'd into shape, a life
in twelve right lines come almost whole.
You were voluntarily committed: you sweat-out hours
to half-know what the day's poems came to.

Who knows what they did? Or,
by your dying, have?
                    Who knows what word
                    you were bringing home?
                    You, bridging marriages,
                    Ulysses into Queens and through.
                    An almost final draft
                    for your collected life,
                    your unrevisable last poem.

IV
You were a trying man, God knows.
Over drinks, or after, your wit mauled,
twice life sized: like your heroic mattress-chest.

Manic, you were brutal. The brightest boy
in school, the school's most cruel monitor,
you wrenched skin, or twisted arms, as if

Caligula were just. Of those who never made
a team, you were Captain; to them, life-long,
you were Boston-loyal. Guilt in excess

was your subject, not your better nature.
For sheer guts you had no peer. Sane,
you almost seemed God's gentlest creature.

V
Jesus, how death gets to us . . .

On the Common, just this week,
they've jacked up Harriet Winslow's house,
all the front sills gone.

And on the sea-side of the Barn
you wrote in, the bulkhead
finally gave way to the tide.

And then the giving-way you,
like Agee, never got to write:
a poet in a New York cab . . .

VI
Weighed by your dying,
Cal, I find myself

much wanting. How could
I dread you less, or

love you more? Left
time, I try to write

old summers back, as if
you'd never maddened

my perspective. More
in misery than love,

I have your life
by heart. Without you,

I am easier and less:
the planet grays,

the village rot
you left eats through

another step, the Bay
that was our commonplace

is flatter . . .

VII
Everything about me
sags: my body tells

my disbelief its
own mortal story.

I mean to write
a different poem:

> A *seal to tides.*
> A *heron lifted off.*
> A *meteor.*

No. If poems
can be believed,

better how
time conjugates:

day by day,
day after day,
this day after yesterday . . .

a dog with flattened
ears, lying on

old dung, lifts
his muzzle, the lame

best that he can,
to welcome his

old master
home.

May all such ghosts attend
your spirit, now. May it,
with them, be lighter.

GATHERING GREENS

Donald Dike (1920–1978)

In thin snow
blown inland
from sea, all

afternoon I've
tracked into
the woods after

cedar, hemlock,
and spruce. I've
come across

mouse-print,
fox-sign, and
deer run to where

the old dark
sends the night.
I've been here

before, but not
so far in; not
beside partridge

in blow-down, not
to the deeryard
in snow. I need

to learn to
protect myself,
as any animal

must. I try
to learn with
myself to be

gentle: to wait
until light
for the first

shadow to
point me out
to the coast.

LICHENS

Close to the point a mile upriver
where nuclear waste begins
to waste, close to the end

of the century, the coast weathers
before its next weather: March,
the primary colors still sky,

ocean, granite, spruce, snow;
and in a noon clearing, a knoll
in woods the British once stormed,

the lichens as the sun finds them:
nonflowering pioneer plants,
a low mix of algae and fungi,

they name themselves: Toad Skin
or Map Lichen written on rock,
Reindeer rampant through moss,

British Soldiers in log rot,
and Pale Shield lichen against
the Northside of hemlock, rooted

where redcoats fell for nothing,
where man availeth not, where
the wind veers quiet as if March

could prime new life, the lichens
still, the lichens hold,
close to the bone of the planet.

THOREAU NEAR HOME

Seasick off Cape Ann, by moonlight,
on the night boat bound for Portland,
he took a week by mailcoach
tacking inland in hope
of some new school that wanted teaching.
No one listened save an Oldtown Indian.

May 13: looking East from Belfast for
some fairer weather, he booked passage
for Castine, an eight-mile reach, aboard
the sailboat *Cinderilla.*

He found the harbor full: coasters, one
square-rigger, shallops, pulling-boats.
Walking Argyle Street's steep hill, he
step by step rested his whole frame,
that each moment might abide. White clapboard,
spires, and cupolas claimed his eye.
A boy named Philip Hooke pointed to
Fort George, meadowy ramparts crowning
the peninsula. A war ago, boys
hardly men were posted here to die.

No, no teaching offered here.
By another spring, he thought, I
may be a Greenland whaler or
mail-carrier in Peru. All answers
being in the future, day answering
to day, he studied, into evening, how
merchants and how seamen paced their lives.
Bright as roadside shadblow

the night came fresh with stars.
He stayed the night at Deborah Orr's.

Captain Skinner, on the morning packet
back to Belfast, kept the poems of Burns
shelved in his cabin. As strewn clouds cleared,
Thoreau took the deck and looked back at the cliffs
that had not heard of Emerson.
The village shone.

Within a week, Thoreau would be home;
two months from now he would be twenty-one.
He stood watch on Castine, the farthest East
he ever sailed. He thought back to the *Iliad* and Homer;
he found the day fit for eternity, and saw
how sunlight fell on Asia Minor.

TREE NURSERY

Infinite rows of calm,
hundreds of sizes of stretch.

Plot upon plot, they give
themselves to the sun to true up.

They ladder the eye.
Colors from spruce to beech.

lilac trying to spring,
maple left gold from fall.

Every one planted to cross
the horizon. Antennae,

arms, hourglasses, arches,
roots inverted to victories:

not one branch in infinity
fails to take its own shape.

▲

All night the wind
says what it says.
Blind to the moment,
I lie back into
the depth of my life,
pretending to know
the trees' translation.

▼

THE VALLEY ROAD

Before eight,
the sun already hours up
into May, the thin
children come out.

Clustered
in front of shut
housetrailer doors,
or farmsteads gone to
dry rot,
        they open
like laughter:
              loose-
strife, bluet, star-
flower, arbutus,
                  early
at every
schoolbus stop.

▲

By self-definition
I cannot measure
a particle of myself,
not even the wavelength
of my own shadow. How
can I shape what I feel?
Beyond naming names,
nothing can help.
I learn my limits,
I write what I can;
I didn't become
a poet for nothing.

▼

EATON'S BOATYARD

To make do, making a living:
                    to throw away nothing,
practically nothing, nothing that may
come in handy:
                    within an inertia of caked paintcans,
frozen C-clamps, blown strips of tarp, and
pulling-boat molds,
                    to be able to find,
for whatever it's worth,
                    what has to be there:
the requisite tool
                    in this culch there's no end to:
the drawshave buried in potwarp,
chain, and manila jibsheets,
                    or, under the bench,
the piece that already may fit
                    the idea it begins
to shape up:
                    not to be put off by split rudders,
stripped outboards, half
a gasket, and nailsick garboards:
                    to forget for good
all the old year's losses,
                    save for
what needs to be retrieved:
                    a life given to
how today feels:
                    to make of what's here
what has to be made
to make do.

▲

Nothing is more than
simple absence: no father,
no tree to lean on,
no current to ride,
no rock off the shore
to feel a toe down to.

Nothing, at bottom,
is to have nothing
at heart: no self left
who will hear one's
other self speak, no
sense that relates
to another sense,
feeling nothing
permeate everything.

Nothing has meaning.
Nothing means what
it says: the acute
presence of absence:
the who I am not,
the where God isn't,
the void the dead leave,
the when I am dead.

Nothing is infinite absence
invading the finite truth
of my life: my own absence
from years of mornings,
the emptying-out of self
I cannot avoid, the void
of not being I cannot
learn to believe in.

▼

BUILDING HER

Wood: learning it:
                    feeling the tree
shiver the helve, feeling the grain
resist the saw, feeling for grain
with adze and chisel, feeling the plank
refuse a plane, the voyage of sap
still live in the fiber;
                    joining wood:
scarfing it, rabbeting keel and sternpost,
matching a bevel, butting a joint
or driving a trunnel:
                    whatever fastens
the grain, the grain lets in, and binds;

let wood breathe or keep wood briny,
wood will outlive generations:

working wood, a man learns how
wood works:
                    wood comes and goes
with weather or waves; wood gives:

come to find right grain for timbers,
keelson, stem, a man can feel
how wood remembers:
                    the hull will
take to sea the way the tree knew wind.

▲

Nothing answers to
nothing. Nothing
else. The question
is not how to outlive
life, but how
—in the time we're
possessed by—to face
the raw beauty of being.

▼

DAYRISE

At first light I hear miles of silence.
Except for the First Selectman's snowtires
snuffling up Main Street, it's Sunday-quiet;

half awake, knowing that deer season's done,
I dream of does wounded, bedded in spruce groves.
And bucks downed in the bog, who had last night

to give up. I doze with Han-Shan, the old T'ang drunk,
who took to Cold Mountain after the capital
turned down his poems. The woodfire's dying;

I get myself up to stoke it, rewrite night-notes
next to the stove, and wake my wife. After breakfast,
before I try to home-in on today's unwritten poem,

we go out into winter to fell next year's wood:
with her small ax and my stuttering saw, we cut near the bog,
on the low spruce crown of the woodlot we call Cold Knoll.

▲

Given this day, none
better, I stretch to
let trees revive me;
I allow the dead
recall themselves;
I behold nothing,
forgive God; I tell
myself to change
be native: I bare
myself, sleep moved
by stars, take dreams
toward morning; I want
with trees to affect
the day: to lend joy,
accept pain, give
without question;
as trees, beyond doubt,
face prevailing light,
I let love wake me:
I extend myself to
every reflection, as
I have to, to feel for
the planet: nowhere
better (with nothing
to lose) than here
to give thanks that
life takes place.

▼

BEFORE SLEEP

The day put away before bed,
the house almost closed before night.

By the time I walk out over the knoll,
down the steep Main Street

that dead-ends in the sea,
the village has put out its lights.

The winter stars are turned up over
the tide, a tide so quiet the harbor

holds stars. The planet holds.
Before the village turns over in sleep,

I stand at the edge of the tide,
letting my feet feel into the hillside

to where my dead ancestors live.
Whatever I know before sleep

surrounds me. I cannot help know.
By blood or illness, gossip or hope,

I'm relative to every last house.
Before I climb home up the hill, I hold:

I wait for myself to quiet, breathing
the breath of sleepers I cannot help love.

THE HOUSE IN THE TREES

Within an island of trees in the space of nature
it is barely there.
                    Hard to discover,
strange to remember the way.
                              The house in the trees
is constantly being arrived at.
It conforms to the hillside, it receives light
as a guest. There is no wind in the trees,
but the house trembles
                        on the verge of being lived in.
It wants paint
                to define its existence, it takes on color
containing the air around it. Walls emerge
in every advent of weather,
                            a house in the process
of being built, of building:
Cézanne said
                I am its consciousness.
Waiting it out, he watched himself making it happen:
within an island of trees, a human
plenitude at the center. This is the house
every day he painted
                        he took to sleep and woke up in,
barely clothed in the freedom of knowing
before it could ever be done
he would have, finally, to leave it.

VII

TO THINK

Suppose the astronomers right:
the original bang, the cosmos

expanding: a fraction less
expansion, the universe would

have collapsed; a fraction more,
gravity wouldn't have held its

stars. But luck, if it was,
made possible biota. We began

to evolve toward wonder: man
on earth. But what if we alone

are conscious, if outside us
there is no measure of our

complexity? Who else could
believe the ways we invent

to see ourselves across time,
to hear across distance, to fire

ourselves into unbreathable sky?
Fire stations, curtainrods,

dogs, zoos, the traffic
down school steps to recess,

the beds we make kids in, the streams
we dam; who, in a cosmos

empty of us, could account for
twi-night baseball or why

we bid Two No Trump or name
a trout fly Blue Cupsuptic?

If only we diagram stars,
and dream them into daylight

as signs of our meaning, as
proof of intent, or hope of

reason beyond our own, what
reason have we to imagine

that anyone might imagine us?
Who, for Christ's sake?

Until we invented God,
who could believe? We love

to believe, we have to believe
we love. But to think:

after we go, in the last
millisecond when boats,

Chicago, tulip beds,
wolves caged in Stuttgart,

incubators, and condoms
all blow, that the planet

will be beyond wonder, without
wonder what we were ever about.

GROWING UP IN KANKAKEE

Irrevocably the day begins our toward each other
turnings.
                    Nurses at their small-town stations in cities
beyond belief, looking for sun at corridor's end
to simply open the day:
                            the day that looks for
that moment as simple as the whole country
seems once to have been:
                            as if this present
could equal the quiet of a man, after years,
standing to speak at Gettysburg;
                            or months
before, the thoughtless quiet of a bluetick hound
at Milledgeville, lifting an ear to how history arrives.

It is simple to think we ever were simple,
even when we were the boy with the camera, standing
where luck would have us, when a three-horse pumper
rounded a corner in Kankakee.
                            Think of whatever morning
it was when Sam Clemens first played hooky in Hannibal,
and thought he might write a book or two
which might finally come to be about
                            who we think now
we always thought we wanted to be.

PUBLIC BROADCAST

Sunday, late. The winter dark already coming down.
Inside the woodshed door, an early FM tuned to Bangor.
Half as old as the backyard oak he's felled—felled,
fitted, split—and old man mad for music lugs the chunks in.
He turns the volume up, up full: an opera he never saw
rises through light snow and marshals its triumphant march.
He marches, lifting stiff knees into highstep, marking
his own bootprints, shooting his victorious fist
against a stand of second growth ranked naked
against the sky. He lets the music take him as
he assumes the music: entering the city gates
he feels the blaze of banners, the shine on breastplates
and the women's hair. He marches near the column's head,
in his just place. The sun on the lead car is hot,
the horses sweat with victory, a victory
he hasn't felt in fifty years. Measure upon measure,
the music pumps him higher. He marches, marches,
through his deep backyard. The chorus soars:
the women's voices open every street, their smiles
are wide with glory, their lips already moist.

DREAMBOAT

Wanting a boat, making the rounds
of boatyards, grounding the dream
of having her, figuring costs,

tying one on at the jazz hole
down by the wharf, as high
as Sea Smoke on *China Boy;*

Taiwan cutters junky with teak,
but Julie (all of eleven last Tuesday),
her father at sea, dancing out

in the street with her mother,
a dreamboat rigged like
a yawl called *Concinnity;*

maybe it's time to order another,
to hoist a few more, over old
Muskrat Ramble, over the blues,

wanting a hull with good sheer
and fine entry, her lines
fair as the riff of the heart

within the crest and lift
of the music, the band surging
on *Maple Leaf Rag,* Julie feeling

her body feel it, the lead trumpet
riding it out, the mind blowing solo
out across the Atlantic.

PROCESSION

A white-throat flicked into the sunset window.
How small a thing to bury: his short neck limp,
eye perfectly blank, the feathers warm in my hand.

Nothing left now to whistle *Old Sam Peabody,*
Peabody, Peabody. . . . The rest in their thickets,
knowing to go. The winter stars coming. Out early

this morning I see Orion, the first time this fall,
Aldebaran brilliant in Taurus, the Dipper's
handle tipped down toward daybreak. As sun-up

dims Venus, I walk the first frost out into ground fog,
as it happens. Slowly, it comes to me: today
would be father's 85th birthday. I hear

today's birds in the cedars, woken, knowing to go.
I think of a boy years beyond me, back in Council Bluffs,
a boy with father's name, out on a third-floor porch

after midnight, without knowing why, watching (he must
have told me hundreds of times) against his own horizon
these same winter stars beginning to show.

A MAN IN MAINE

North. The bare time.
The same quick dark
from Rutland to Nome,

the utter chill.
Winter stars. After
work, splitting birch

by the light outside
his back door, a man
in Maine thinks what

his father told him,
splitting outside
this same back door:

every November, his
father said, he thought
when he split wood

of what his father
said the night he
right here died: just

after supper, his
father said, his father
came out back, looked

out at the sky
the way he had
for years, picked up

his ax, struck
the oak clean, and
was himself struck

down; before he
died he just had
this to say:

this time of
year the stars
come close some fierce.

SMALL TOWN

You know.
        The light on upstairs
before four every morning. The man
asleep every night before eight.
What programs they watch. Who
traded cars, what keeps the town
moving.
        The town knows. You
know. You've known for years over
drugstore coffee. Who hurts, who
loves.
        Why, today, in the house
two down from the church, people
you know cannot stop weeping.

BEYOND EQUINOX

The sailboats hauled, their seasonal moorings
towed to mudflat coves; the summer cottages
closed and boarded. Beyond equinox, the short days
let their light back into native lives.
                              White clapboard
clean as November, the strict lawns raked;
sunset angles again to the granite foundations.
Then months of wind: all day out of the North,
all night with the weight of cold behind it.
Behind Bucksport a partridge buries her ruff
in first snow, and settles in.
                              Up in black dark
to stoke her woodstove, a Water Street widow
turns on the light. She feels how her body has,
by her clothes, been slighted, how her house
no longer fits. Taking her bearings with all
due caution, carefully she thinks to herself:
Where are we when we think? With no one to answer
she speaks aloud: *Inside ourselves, looking out
for our lives.*
                              As the fire catches, her housecat wakes.
Morning keeps coming: the harbor out the window
clears to new whitecaps. Daylong, watching, she
and her cat move from room to room with the sun.

FIRE ON THE ISLAND

People, on their safe shore, two miles
away, look out at the island as if
they were wondering what it all meant.
As if, if they knew how it started,
the fire might end like a poem they once
tried to learn; *Water, water,*
everywhere. . . . But nobody knows
how it started. Everyone asks. But
then they get back to *Nobody knows.*
Maybe the corner behind the old stove.
Or sun, through a bullseye bottle
focused on an old couch. Who can tell?
Whatever happened, there it is:
the smoke plumed, the flame grown, until
even the mainland can see it, two miles
away. Now the whole side of the house,
the old gray shingles catching,
fire climbing the trellis where once
there must have been roses. Next to
the woodshed, now, the dead spruce
become a huge torch. Now the whole house,
the fire beginning to top. The way
the wind is, the whole island.
The whole island, for sure. *For*
sure, they say on the mainland,
the way people say. *But what*
can you do, they keep saying.
A schoolkid keeps wanting to know
Why don't they try to save it?
A girl who's getting ready for
college has barely started to say

No way when the whole sky
over the island blows. Maybe only
a propane tank, maybe some stored
explosive. Whatever it was,
there's a different smoke. But no
sound at all, on the mainland.
The way the wind was, the report
must have blown out to sea.
Jesus, an old man says, *she's*
gone for good now. The girl
half hugs herself: *That really*
blew me away. I mean it could.
It could blow you away. And . . .
Already the sky looks half clear.
No, the old man says, *no And.*
Right there's the whole of it.
But nobody knows for sure
what the whole of it means.
However it started, or whatever
blew, there's no telling now
whose words began to come close.
Whatever they once were wondering,
the people have all gone into
their houses. The island is where
it always was, alive in
its own low smouldering.

SPECIES

For seasons beyond count, age
after age, through generations,
they watched us, naked of eye,

through every possible lens:
we were pictured, widely, as
of more or less intelligence.

They measured our migrations,
guessed at the code in our blood,
the tidal pull of the sun,

or what the stars told us.
In weather when we spoke clearly
what they only partially sensed,

they knew to tape our voices;
they collected how they thought
we spoke. Or sang. Of how

we spoke they wrote music.
To our habitats, fieldmarks, even
our habits of pairing, they made

themselves guides. They saw
in us an endangered species;
they listed us with governments.

Out of guilt for the hunting,
even long after, or for what
we barely reminded them of,

we believe they almost loved us.
What we can never know is
how we failed to let them feel

what we meant in our deepest instinct,
in the great dance of our silence.
At the latitudes where we winter,

we only know to gather, to sing
to our young and ourselves, warning
after warning of how they became extinct.

OVER ANTARCTICA

So. After years of plans and logistics,
here we are finally: at the high latitudes

far to the South, running low on everything,
but otherwise setting some kind of record,

flying a not small plane against the spin
of the planet. We circumnavigate close

to the Pole, close to what we dreamt
as its infinite stillness. It's gone,

whatever it was: the dream, the world,
the dream of a world; it's as much lost to us

as we are to it. Over and over, as we
home in on an absence, the instruments spin:

we swirl and churn in our own debris,
from Point No Point back to Point No Point.

STONINGTON

Fog come over us.
Come under sea wind
over cold tide, fog

blown home against
the sharp ebb. Fog
at the harbor bell.

Fog on the headland.
Fog in the goldenrod,
fog at the fishwharves,

come over the island.
Fog tall in spruce,
feeling inland; a soft

quiet on porches, fog
after dark; in small bedrooms,
the harbor bell close.

Spruce full of fog,
fog all this night,
come over all of us.

TABLE

Before he died, he thought,
he might let someone know
how his own life felt;
　　　　　　　but when he looked
to turn out the light, he saw
on his table how things, by way
of his own unwritten will, had already
arranged themselves:
　　　　　　　a photograph of
his wife some forty years since;
　　　　　　　　　the standard editions
of what he took to be Thoreau's and Melville's
prime hymns; a taped-up paperback called
Character and Opinion, which half-explained
almost everything;
　　　　　　　his own spiral-bound dreamlog
(its tonight's entries still wanting);
a radio, after hours of Bach,
pretuned to tomorrow's weather;
　　　　　　　a marked copy
of Valéry's *Aesthetics*; the portable
Chekhov; and a first-draft poem of the poet
whose work most touched him.
　　　　　　　He had the presence
of mind to leave these matters
as they self-presented.
　　　　　　　He slept
with helical dreams, and woke at first light
to hear rain on the roof, to watch
the scud of low nimbus,
　　　　　　　and then to focus-in

as he reached to the table for
his bifocals:
                    to find again in the still life there
an issue of something more than itself,
the more and other that over and over
recalled him, the other and all
to which he woke beholden:
                                and this day
meant again to try to give thanks to, if
he could, for the life of him, join, and return,
any words that might measure.

SAYING IT

Saying it. Trying
to say it. Not
to answer to

logic, but leaving
our very lives open
to how we have

to hear ourselves
say what we mean.
Not merely to

know, all told,
our far neighbors;
or here, beside

us now, the stranger
we sleep next to.
Not to get it said

and be done, but to
say the feeling, its
present shape, to

let words lend it
dimension: to name
the pain to confirm

how it may be borne:
through what in
ourselves we dream

to give voice to,
to find some word for
how we bear our lives.

Daily, as we are daily
wed, we say the world
is a wedding for which,

as we are constantly
finding, the ceremony
has not yet been found.

What wine? What bread?
What language sung?
We wake, at night, to

imagine, and again wake
at dawn to begin: to let
the intervals speak

for themselves, to
listen to how they
feel, to give pause

to what we're about:
to relate ourselves,
over and over; in

time beyond time
to speak some measure
of how we hear the music:

today if ever to
say the joy of trying
to say the joy.

AFTER THE REBUILDING

After the rebuilding was done, and
the woodstove finally installed, after
the ripping-out of walls, tearing back to
its beams the house he'd lived in, frozen, for over
fifty years, he started mornings up with the world's
most expensive kindling. Not just scraps of red oak from
new flooring, ends of clear birch from kitchen trim, and
knots from #2 pine, but oddlot pieces of his old life:
window frames clawed from his daughter's lost room,
his grandfather's coat peg, shelving his mother
had rolled her crust on, and lathing first plastered
the year Thoreau moved to Walden. The woodstove itself
was new: the prime heat for four new rooms descended
from seven, the central logic for all the opening up,
for revisions hammered out daily, weeks of roughing-in,
and after months of unfigured costs, the final bevels
and the long returning. Oh, when he first got up to
rekindle the fire of November mornings, he found
that everything held heat: he sweat as he tossed
the chunks in; he found himself burning, burning.

EVENING

Evening: the fog rides in over small woods,
unrolling onto the garden made from the field.

In the house, the boy who planted the garden
takes his turn at putting together supper. The father,

who rented the house to have his time with the boy,
picks volunteer phlox by the edge of the woods.

The fog feels like rain, the garden needs sun. The boy
sets the table with spoons, then tosses three kinds

of lettuce, chopped scallions, spinach, and lots
of sliced cucumbers into a bowl. He passes his father

the ketchup. They sit on the two chipped chairs without
saying the blessing; the flowers the father put in a jar

grace the table. They have another week left.
Except for having to finish the postcard he's almost

written his mother, the boy is happy. Watching him
pour more ketchup onto his salad, his father

invents another new face. The boy grins.
His father points to the postcard; he washes up

by himself while the boy writes his mother.
Then his father reads the next chapter he promised.

The fog is all but asleep in the woods, evening
deepens the house; August has settled over the garden

the man and his son dug in June from the field.

A TWO INCH WAVE

The sea, flat
               on a coming tide:
a two inch wave
                  climbs the low sand,
drags, curls,
              and topples.
Over and over,
                the water toppling
gathers and
             gains on itself.
It tempts us,
             whoever it is
we think we are,
              to humanize
comparisons
             —but that belongs
to another
            century's nonsense.
Only the semi-
             palmated plovers,
feeding in mid-
             migration, two
strong, claim
            the advancing edge
as their own:
             they dip quick beaks
at something
             we cannot pretend
to see;
         inshore of ducks
floating calm,

off-tide of oaks
growing tall,
between the field
of a field
and the field of the
incoming sea,
they dip quick beaks
into a margin
we cannot fathom;
they strike for
a sustenance only
they know. We
only partially
guess. The planet,
maybe
the cosmos,
they share with us,
or we share
with them, is a mystery
not to be solved;
what is here, now,
is *here, now,*
beyond every knowledge
except our caring:
fetched from behind
the old sun,
in the huge blue over us still,
Arcturus and all
her proximate stars
are already bound
to brighten and seem
to rise, as they
even now tip to ebb,
angled into the sea
on their own inviolate wavelength.

RELATIONS
Old Light/New Sun/Postmistress/Earth/04421

From broken dreams,
                    we wake to every day's
brave history,

the gravity
            of every moment
we wake

to let our lives
                inhabit: *now, here, again,*
this very day,

passionate as all
                  Yeats woke in old age
to hope for, the sun

turns up, under
                an offshore cloudbank
spun at 700 and

some mph to meet it,
                    rosy as the cheeks
of a Chios woman

Homer may have been
                    touched by, just
as Janet

is touching, climbing
                      familiar steps, granite
locally quarried,

to work at 04421,
                    a peninsular village
spun, just as

Janet is spun,
                    into light, light appearing
to resurrect

not simply its own
                    life but the whole
improbable

system, tugging
                    the planet around to
look precisely

as Janet looks,
                    alight with the gravity
of her office,

before turning
                    the key that opens up
its full

radiance:
          the familiar arrivals,
departures,

and even predictable
                    orbits in which,
with excited

constancy, by how
                    to each other
we're held, we keep

from spinning out
                    by how to each other
we hold.

VIII

GARDEN

Went to a man in
his patch of garden.

Knew his brother was
in for surgery

over to the V.A.
Heard at the store

his sister, the
one that he'd

kept home forever,
died. Heard he

had to shoot his
dog the same day.

Told him I was
sorry, what

could I say. He
never spoke of the

sister; said when
he got up this

morning he saw
his dog couldn't,

said, *she was*
parallel from

the waist down.
His old eyes

wanted tears; mine
felt them come. Could

feel him feeling
how *Addie was*

parallel, up
in her head, from

when she was
born. He bent,

of a sudden,
folded himself

to grab some
old broccoli out

of his patch. And
stayed down, half-

kneeling. I tried
to stay, looking

around the garden
and, over the edge

of the world, out
at all the old sky.

ZEROS

Three zeros coming up,
as the odometer turns
toward its new thousand.
Old movies, cars, pushing
2002, the number maybe
we'll get to, maybe we'll
not. As if numbers were
our destination, as if
we weren't close to lost.
As if it didn't matter
how we've already poisoned
the planet, invaded lovers,
born generations of micro-
chips, wired our lives to
suicide bombs, and still
told ourselves, year after
penultimate year, that there
will be survivors, that we'll
be the heroes who'll last.

GAME

Between periods,
                    boys at the urinals,
boymen, menboys, telling AIDS jokes,
yelling *Ain't the game great.*
                              Jesus,
'djou see 'em rack that one up
right at the goal . . .
                         Freshman girls
in the stands,
                    screaming at referees
their fathers' utmost obscenities.
They must have learned
                         in the womb,
here or in Rome, at some earlier series,
limp but awake, the way,
                         in their parents' arms,
tonight's kids are fallen.
                         The other side
of the glass partition
                    the hurt players lie,
scattered like death at Antietam,
the trainers working over them, working
them over,
                    to get them back in the game.
O, its sheer violence,
                         our innate violence,
my anger squared in that tight arena
until I could not speak, or stay, but
walked myself out into winter sky,
                              out through
a door where a woman stamped me

with an ink pinetree,
                        sure,
since I'd paid so much,
I would come back in.

CIVILITIES

Kids in the city, where
there are only dogs, all
the time yelling it.
The same as country kids
yell, trying to be
tough; or women, proving
they have the same right
as men. Rich men pretending
they farm. None of them
within range of my grandmother,
whose proud Victorian bowels
never grumbled, who knew
right words, and which
to use when.
           When Mr. Bowden
brought to her garden
cartloads of spring dressing,
it was presented, and
billed, as such. In her
presence, horse manure
was not a phrase he'd think
to use. Not that he didn't,
being from up in The County,
know deer droppings from
moosescat, or bearscat
from fox-sign.
           Fifty years gone,
this tilt backyard is still weighed
by their presence: Mr. Bowden
and Mrs. Hooke, bald pate
and ample bosom, their joined

civilities out inspecting
the edged border of her
perennial garden—the same
garden I'm just about to
turn over for turnips, beets,
and squash, being myself,
in the quick of spring,
already up to my boottops
in the back of the pickup,
forking out to my wife
lovely dark clods of cowdung.

FALLBACK

An outdoor sign: under the big word FARVIEW
smaller letters spell *Intermediate Care.*

Year-round, now, she focuses at first light
on the sign, a wren of a woman looking out
from her cover. The night girl wakes her
at six for a washcloth, before
the day girls come on.
                              In the waking
they've shared for sixty-two years, she watches
Stanton getting his face washed, next to
the window in the same room. Out the windows, over
the sign, rain thickens the lake, clouds
lie low on the mountain.
                              My body gone,
she thinks, *and his mind.*
                              When anyone visits,
his manners rise from the room's one armchair,
in his tweed suit, intact; she lies back
where she's been all day, her backbone so thin
the doctor jokes that X-rays can't find it.
She thinks her daughter may come today.
If she can. Labor Day she couldn't. Today
it's almost Hallowe'en, the Day Room filled
with paper pumpkins. Down at the nurse's station
the girls have carved a real one.
                              Out the window
not much color: the oaks dead bronze,
the marshgrass rusty. This morning she plans
how to set their watches tonight:
the old rule: *spring forward,*

fall back.
		Now the night girl is back,
saying she's doing a double shift, covering
for Elsie.
		And the loons have been fewer, out
on the lake, and the Red Delicious are far
from what they were. Even at home,
the last year Elmer brought manure,
he said *Somethin's wrong with the bees,*
they're not comin round to spread pollen.
She watches Stanton wanting to talk to
the girl while she cranks up his bed;
watching, his curtain all the way back,
she can see his pale emeritus head risen into
the steel engraving of Harvard College.
						His mind,
she thinks, *and my body.*
					Bringing trays now,
the night girl looks like a grebe. The woman
sips tea. Watching her husband try cereal,
she thinks back to summers they bird-watched,
Julys on Monhegan, a week once on Skye.
					. . . *out-of-*
style beyond doubt, we were worn but fit.
His old Harris jacket, scratchy only in places.
She tries to smell the peat smell, the jacket he
laid out for picnics. But the night girl, bending
to take her tray, brings her home: the perfume
still lingering from whatever went on
before last night's shift.
				And you at twenty,
who look away from us, wearing so cleverly little
(she smiles an idle small smile at her husband)
—how would you know we ever made love
in the sweetfern high on an island.

CALLING

Across the bay, under its heavy Northwest sky,
horizon strips of deep light leaving the day.

The man on the shore stands in his own weather,
recalled by the light's low angle to the same sky,

the day years ago they scattered his father's ashes
across the Platte. He tries to figure how far today is

from the solstice. His watch shows two days to go,
and 4:06. *In another fifty-four minutes the rates*

will go down. He turns back home, sure beyond doubt:
I ought to call father. It's time I called father.

HEADING OUT

Beyond here there's no map.
How you get there is where
you'll arrive; how, dawn by
dawn, you can see your way
clear: in ponds, sky, just as
woods you walk through give
to fields. And rivers: beyond
all burning, you'll cross on bridges
you've long lugged with you.
Whatever your route, go lightly,
toward light. Once you give away
all save necessity, all's
mostly well: what you used to
believe you owned is nothing,
nothing beside how you've come
to feel. You've no need now
to give in or give out: the way
you're going your body seems
willing. Slowly as it may
otherwise tell you, whatever
it comes to you're bound to know.

RULE ONE

Rule One of all
rules one:
        No one ever knows
how much another hurts.
              You.
Kate. Ray. Randall. Me.
           The nurses
who were kind to you, the gaspump kid
across the bridge, the waitress here
this noon.
        No one ever knows.
Or maybe in a thousand, one
has the toughness to,
            to care,
to give beyond a selfish pity. Even
any given day,
          given weathers, detours,
chances of what look like luck,
if we feel bad
         we refuse the givens.
What blighted lives we lead.
             Or follow:
showering, feeding, changing shirts or
pants, working, as one used to say,
to make ourselves presentable.
              Partial
strangers to our painful selves,
we're still stranger to
diminished friends
when they appear
to hurt.

How much we fail them,
failing to come close:
                    a parent,
newly single, in Seattle;
an upstate poet in intensive care.
You. Blanche. Alvin. Sue.
                    Who hurts
and why.
          Why we guess we know.
How much we never.

AMONG HOUSES

Among houses, none an adequate windbreak
for any other, a cold house
on a cold harbor, the Labrador current
icing its spilings on every tide.

Time seeps away. As nights gather,
the same argument over and over,
the last twenty years empty as Christmas.
Neither one what the other wants.

One day of sun and twelve of overcast,
the relentless nimbus of wanting change,
but the same wind picking at chinks,
the same small house grown smaller.

The emotions of shut-ins. They've insulated
to no avail: he will not let her be,
she will not let him feel. The old wind
catches its breath and starts in.

Christ, she thinks, *in my lifetime
has not risen. I continue to miss Him.*
He in his corner stiffens: *Who was I
before I went numb? Who did we used*

to be? They sleep separate dreams
and eat the same breakfast, same cold argument:
one day of argument, twelve of truce;
the same newspaper stuffed in chinks,

the same plastic tacked over the window.
Miles of drift-ice close in on the coast,
the world gone over the edge with sunset,
nothing to speak of left.

DARK

He knocked. He could hear her
come to the door.
Then, when it opened, there
was nobody there.

DIRECTIONS

Imagine your insuranceman figuring how to say
the absence of imagination has to be imagined.
Now, without a vestige of laughter, presume to imagine
two people getting their bodies together: literally
scratching each other's back, touching this, feeling
for that, playing their tongues, their fingers, reaching
there or here, even using their toes, *and not laughing?*
Imagine not telling small lies into one ear or another;
or after due seasons, not smiling behind one's closed eyes.
Imagine, in fact, the comedy of a man making love to a woman,
making love over and over, for years, with a woman for whom
what's around the next corner, even on roads near home,
is repeatedly new, who joyfully forgets directions of
every kind; a woman for whom imagination is as simple
as Eden, as when, come early to bed, she sees a man in Augusta
sink a long putt on a black-and-white green on TV, and asks
of her husband, to his constant amazement, *Can you imagine?*

SIXTY

Spring hills, dark contraries:
a glade in a fall valley,
its one flower steeped with sun.

The there and here of her.
The soft where.
The sweet closeness when.

From dreams awake to turn to her.
Remembering, remembering.
And now again. Again.

SEEING

*Ansel Adams postcards
from Maine to Kansas
and back*

Far west of here
the dark foothills,
the high Sierra ridged
behind them. In a near field
a horse dark as hills,
grazing light.
                    I say
on my postcard *a glory
of mountains, the mystery
of light absolute.*
You say, by airmail
from halfway to there
from here, *I see
what you mean.*
                    You
who have been there:
the dark above pasture,
the snowfields above
the whole world; you
say you see and, after
love, sign your
simplest name.
                    Who
can I be to think to
scale mountains,
to think how mountains
lend scale to the hills,
and how both are lent scale
by the horse?

                    Who
can say how far
a man longs, after all
he is not, toward
all his want. I cannot
bear to. I only know,
far to the East, how
I know light and know
dark:
          whenever I
write you, you who've
never been here
where I am, I
see you, who cannot
know all you mean,
cantering that dark horse
across a small orchard,
the very small orchard
outside this back window.

WORDS MADE FROM LETTERS

Letters made of words, mailed letters
thickly definite.
              But oh, to talk,
not to but with. Not stamps or phone,
but having made some harbor: say long after
dinner, and still longer; or walking
fields before:
                   along stonewalls, a high field's
cold geometries in the small new snow.
Evenings, in each other's eyes, seeing
what gets said: the feel of words
we didn't know we knew to say, but found
we had, and did.
              Odd words like *lie-lows,* or
say, *souvenirs,* as they come to mind from letters
written in a rainy light: like photographs,
not dark from absent knowledge, but caringly
made lucent: the way you tell how foxes greet
by *gekkering.*
             Foxes met in your fields' Butterwort,
no doubt, or Bishop's Weed—on the hilly margin
where your eyelids ache to sleep, and
maybe dream a February story:
                       how wooden yawls,
cradled rail to rail in their great boatshed,
far up Center Harbor, all winter whisper to
each other how the summer went.
                   I hear you
as I read you, fingertip to fingertip against
the same gray page: the cadences of seasons,
your dogs' tails giving hearthroom to

the thump of your own heart.

                                    I read you
soft and clear, even when, by card,
you write me from the Rockies to
reread *Job 38*. All that mountain power
and distance, yes. Rereading, I hear
Roethke's perfect theft of *Hath the rain
a father?*

                    And back to you I offer:
Who hath put wisdom in the inward parts?
Or who hath given understanding to the heart?
God knows I cannot bind the Pleiades, nor
can you loose Orion's bands.

                                    We make do with
old words and new:

                                    Mesenteries, you write back
from weeks ago, you learned from your dead father
thirty falls before, drawing birds he'd shot,
asking, as you reached two fingers in,

                                    *How come
the guts and giblets all come out a piece?*
You say now he said

                                    Mesenteries,
these pale visceral tissues which hold all in place,
which film these opalescent works so brightly coiled
in what you now recall as

                                    death's own vegetable smell.
Well, we're bound to that,

                                    in truth. But while
there's time I want to write I'm glad
to be alive in the same world as you,

                                    here where
there's, yes, a wisdom in the inward parts,
where something mesenteric loosely binds us,
where you, as words are bound to tell,
have given understanding to my heart.

MARCHES

Sun just up on the century's earliest equinox;
patchy snow in the woods, ice not yet out,
woodcock migrating into the alder thickets.
Far from woodsheds with less than a dry cord left,

the young winter-out on their counter-migrations:
wading the surf, getting wasted, pretending
they cannot die, and will not, as long as
their bodies tan, and burn to feel each other's.

Far in the desert, out to arrest their government,
twelve hundred women and men, hands linked against
a chainlink fence, give themselves to arrest.
Handcuffed, shunted to barbedwire camps, they delay

the test for twenty-four hours. In which new day
thousands of death-needles are passed, uncountable
lovers die shunned by their parents, hundreds of
children are born with systems in no way immune.

And millions of the rest of us, self-righteous
in the perfect democracy of backcountry roads, freeways,
and interstates, pass each other at life-span speeds;
or close, in opposing lanes, at a hundred-and-thirty,

trusting implicitly in simple self-interest, missing
each other, time after time, only by fragments of seconds,
as we move our lives, or dyings, another round toward
what March may be like in maybe the year 2000.

PROVISIONS

The paperback somebody left on the plane
tells what you'll need to carry on your person:
immune seeds in a shielded packet, something of value
to barter, a hardener to refill your own teeth.
The book suggests what weapon to take against
your own kind. And the canteen of water from
pipes still safe; salve for your skin;
a drug, at any cost, against immediate pain.
You already know you won't want for matches;
you will have thought, long since, of boots
with impervious soles, fit for the distance;
repellent clothes, a balaclava, or thick-brimmed
hat, toward whatever the season may be.
Proud flesh will be your least of crises,
but take curved scissors for what you'll need
to debride. And, yes, dried food, for twice as long
as you think. The book says *Go, leave objects behind.*
That much is true. Leave the book first of all;
it forgets to say what you cannot forget: that there's
no place to go. Whether or not you go or stay, make
an eyeshield, pocket next to your heart whatever
poems you might now think to copy, keep with you
what's left of Thoreau. And since no one
but Bach can hold in mind all the Bach
one is bound to need, you might well practice
carrying his simplest tune: the small dance in G
that Anna Magdalena every morning sang
to ease her firstborn son. Carry that music, always,
in your head. What memory you have is all you'll have left;
in whatever mornings there are, you'll have for as long
as you possibly can simply to hum to yourself.

THANKSGIVING

In the beginning was
with Mother,
           swum into her sea,
perfect.
          *

        After, not, save
when she let.
          *

        Then lilac buds, fields
to wander, woods full of names she gave
to touch, to be touched by: hepatica
and bloodroot, dogtooth, trillium;
all April there to hold in eye, then
appleblossoms at floodtide,
                the way a girl
and boy, embodied by each other.
          *

Under trees, arrived to know, no more
to wonder what the wonder is. Held then,
letting wonder hold: the weather where
love happens, a room with all it houses.
          *

A morning season, lasting weeks or seasons,
even years turned in to lives.
              With family,
blood or no, the hard old gentleness,
the gentle wearing down. Or out.
As who'd not guess, within one's self,
endeared by loss to living how it goes.
          *

The long becoming, then becoming gone.
How? Back into where?
                          Barely having grown
toward love: hating
                      to lose any measure.
How leave? How stay
                        what's left? No way
save the old ways,
                        always: not giving in
but to, and being so returned.
                          *
                          And turned,
too, into memory, becoming
finally gray withal. Yet gentle, gentled,
feeling one's self felt in generations
barely born,
                    the way a blind pianist
feels dark music, joyful as he jazzes
how it feels: how all, befallen
finally, rise within us,
                        woken in us,
nightly, when we let them come.
                          *
                        Father,
here at heart, where I have you, you
beyond all want but yearning inward to
be part, again to be embodied:
                              as in
a grandson's eyes,
                    as you through me here are,
given this Thanksgiving:
                          this yearly day,
                        this table where
a daughter's husband, asked to ask the blessing,
gathers hands beside him to complete the ring,

214

quotes Emily here in Amherst and invites us all,
blessed by tears and laughter, to share with her
           . . . a sunny mind,
Thy windy will to bear.

*

                Here where we
bear each other, in us each
the heart beats its small code:
                        so far

so good, so far so
good, so far . . .
                for now, for
now, we give up tears
and, being gathered, sing.

PRESENCE

after George Oppen

That we are here: that we can question who
we are, where; that we relate to how deer

once small have grown bold in our back garden;
that we can ask, ask even ourselves, how

to the other we may appear, here in the always near place
we seem to ourselves to inhabit, who sleep toward

and wake from steeped hills, the sea opening into our eyes
the infinite possibility of infinity

we believe we're neither beyond nor shy of,
here as we are, without doubt, amid then, there,

and now, falling through dark into light, and back,
against which we cannot defend, wish as we might, as we do.

Still, as the physicist said, *the mystery is*
that we are here, here at all, still bearing with,

and borne by, all we try to make sense of:
this evening two does and a fawn who browse

the head lettuce we once thought was ours.
But no. As we chase them off mildly, and make

an odd salad of what they left us, the old stars
come casually out, and we see near and far we own nothing:

it's us who belong to all else; who, given this day,
are touched by, and touch, our tenderest knowing,

our lives incalculably dear as we feel for each other,
our skin no more or less thin than that of redwing,

rainbow, star-nose, or whitethroat, enfolded like us
in the valleys and waves of this irrefutable planet.

IX

FIRST NIGHT

Breathing the wonder. Easing
to breathe. Breath by breath, each
with each other: timing the rise,
floating the fall. Together, together,
letting sleep come.
      Keeping and
keeping, dreaming such sleep.
Sleeping to wake: letting light
wake you, letting the daybreak
hold and behold you, self and
other, together and each.

REQUIESCAT: WESTERN UNION

The yellow pads. The cream walls
and varnished counter. The pencil
on its bright chain: how bluntly

it made the words up, counted them,
then—a quick second blank—
copied them down. Knowing to whom

it was going, how far the sender went
before handing it over: handing it
always to the thin clerk, the man

who figured the cost in his head
before he sat back at his keyboard
to peck out all the emotion.

NAVIGATION

Far inland, he
follows the Dipper's
farside pointers
up to Polaris, turns
90° to starboard,
sights down to
Capella, barely
showing above
the low mountains;
his eye, climbing
from there, finds
Cassiopeia, and off
the angled back
of her chair, again
drops to Mirfak,
a dim star in
Perseus, which will,
as the planet re-
volves into dark, give
him his course
to Aldebaran, the
star, if he ever
sails offshore, he
nightly figures
to navigate by.

PREPOSITIONS

The first race he
scratched from,
        a girl
he didn't go out with,
hills he was never
on top of;
       a bet
he refused to take up,
strangers he wouldn't
move toward, leaves he
didn't turn over:
          the boxcar
he didn't climb into,
weathers he failed
to ride out, stars he
still hasn't sailed by,
and poems he couldn't
wake up for;
        poems and
poems he has yet to
work through:
        After, he says,
I get out from under.

LOOKING

Looking for who she
might be the rest of

her life, she found
her face, three or two

new times a day, in
her mirror, trying

to figure how far
the face looking back

at her face might be
from the face she

was looking in with,
a face with more nose

than she liked. She
watched her face with

no makeup on. Giving
herself the eye, she

saw her face wanting
to know if the woman

deep in the glass was
one foot or two feet

away from the *I*
she dreamt to revise,

the *I* she meant to
give back to her life,

once she found some rule
that might measure

how close to herself she
might let herself come.

PLACES WITHOUT NAMES

Ilion: besieged ten years. Sung hundreds more, then
written down: how force makes corpses out of men.
Men whose spirits were, by war, undone: Salamis,

Shiloh, Crécy. Lives going places gone. Placenames
now, no faces. Sheepmen sent to Passchendaele:
ever after, none could sleep. Barely thirty years:

sons like fathers gone back to the Marne. Gone again to
Argonne Forest, where fathers they could not remember
blew the enemy apart, until they got themselves

dismembered. Sons, too, shot. Bull Run, Malvern Hill:
history tests. Boys who knew left foot from right
never made the grade. No rolls kept. Voices lost,

names on wooden crosses gone to rot. Abroad,
in rivers hard to say, men in living memory
bled their lives out, bodies bloating far downstream.

On Corregidor, an island rock of fortress caves,
tall men surrendered to small men: to each other
none could speak. Lake Ladoga, the Barents Sea, and Attu:

places millhands froze, for hours before they died.
To islands where men burned, papers gave black headlines:
Guadalcanal. Rabaul. Saipan. Iwo. Over which

men like torpedoes flew their lives down into the Pacific.
Tidal beaches. Mountain passes. Holy buildings
older than this country. Cities. Jungle riverbends.

Sealanes old as seawinds. Old villages where,
in some foreign language, country boys got laid.
Around the time the bands start up again, memory

shuts down, each patriot the prisoner of his own flag.
What gene demands old men command young men to die?
The young gone singing to Antietam, Aachen, Anzio.

To Bangladore, the Choisin Reservoir, Dien Bien Phu,
My Lai. Places in the heads of men who have no
mind left. Our fragile idiocy: inflamed five times

a century to take up crossbows, horsepower, warships,
planes, and rocketry. No matter what the weapons,
the dead could not care less. Beyond the homebound wounded

only women, sleepless women, know the holy names:
bed-names, church-names, placenames buried in their
sons' or lovers' heads. Stones without voices,

save the incised name. Poppies, stars, and crosses:
the poverty of history. A wealth of lives. Ours, always
ours: their holy names, those sacrilegious places.

BACKCOUNTRY

Fields between woodlots
touched by frost, small ponds
skimmed with black ice. And
Snow apples, bright
on December branches,
hung out over the sudden curve
on a road where a farm
once was.
           I stop to
name them, named not for
the bright of their skin
but the snow inside; you
nod further on to
the mute gold of Russets,
the sky above both of us
blue beyond blue.
           You go
for a Russet, best keeper
of all. I pull down
a Snow, knowing how short
its shelf-life, and hand
it over, bright as Venus
in this month's dawnings.
You trade me the Russet's
sharp meat for the Snow's
veined white, your smile
as low as the solstice sun.
And why not?
           Why are we
traveling if not to slow,
to make our own waystops?

Why here if not to
wake to the planets, name
winter fruit, and harvest,
for once, how history
tastes on each other's lips.

PAIRS

Years now, good days
more than half the year,

they row late afternoons
out through the harbor

to the bell, a couple
with gray hair, an old

green rowboat. Given sun,
their four oars, stroke

by stroke, glint wet,
so far away that even

in light air their
upwind voices barely

carry. No words translate
to us on shore, more

than a mile from where
they pull and feather.

All we hear is how,
like sea-ducks, they

seem constantly to
murmur. And even

after summer's gone,
as they row out or

home, now and again
we hear, we cannot help

but hear, their years
of tidal laughter.

TALK ABOUT WALKING

Where am I going? I'm going
out, out for a walk. I don't
know where except outside.
Outside argument, out beyond
wallpapered walls, outside
wherever it is where nobody
ever imagines. Beyond where
computers circumvent emotion,
where somebody shorted specs
for rivets for airframes on
today's flights. I'm taking off
on my own two feet. I'm going
to clear my head, to watch
mares'-tails instead of TV,
to listen to trees and silence,
to see if I can still breathe.
I'm going to be alone with
myself, to feel how it feels
to embrace what my feet
tell my head, what wind says
in my good ear. I mean to let
myself be embraced, to let go
feeling so centripetally old.
Do I know where I'm going?
I don't. How long or far
I have no idea. No map. I
said I was going to take
a walk. When I'll be back
I'm not going to say.

LINESQUALL

So much upwelling in the sky.
Fair-weather cumulus for hours,
then thickening haze, two states away

from where the front was forecast.
Then this first cell: the cloudwall
building black, topping out at

maybe twenty thousand, in waves
blown sharp as whitecaps. So much
upwelling heat, such updrafts as

charge lightning to let go. Or lift
old tides and farmponds up until,
reformed, they fall back down, given in

to gravity as hail or linesquall rain.
Lightning now; now the first
big drops. We get up, get back in

the truck, still hot. Even with both
sidevents cracked, the windshield fogs;
the downpour blinds the bridge we crossed

to be so stormed. So much fallout from
such quick upwelling. How map our two ways home?
We wait, to calm. There is, for now, no telling.

TERMS

On land any length of rope that's hitched
to something beyond itself and takes
the strain is called the standing part.
Tossed over a beam or limb, with a slipknot
tied in the farther end, the standing part
could be said to end in a noose. At sea,
put to use, rope changes its name to line.
The part spliced into an eye or, say,
made fast to a shackle, the part that does
the work, that works, remains the standing part.
Any loop or slack curve in the running part
of the line, the part that's not working, becomes
a bight; and the part of the running part
that's let go, or finally eased off
until there's no reserve left, is known
as the bitter end. As it is in other events,
ashore or at sea, that come to the end of the line.

HOPE

Old spirit, in and beyond me,
keep and extend me. Amid strangers,
friends, great trees and big seas breaking,
let love move me. Let me hear the whole music,
see clear, reach deep. Open me to find due words,
that I may shape them to ploughshares of my own making.
After such luck, however late, give me to give to
the oldest dance. . . . Then to good sleep,
and—if it happens—glad waking.

HALF-LIFE

3:00 a.m. Back
from the bathroom,
I've lain awake
for an hour. I
was all right at
2:00, most of me's
still O.K. My feet
are down at the end
of the bed, they and
my head and testicles
still seem to be
the right size. But
my hands, clamped
shut like a baby's
fist, are big as
a catcher's mitt,
each thumb's as big
as a fat man's leg.
I can't get any
sound up from my
throat. I grab
for breath, trying
to cry out.
       Though
she has been dead
for half my life,
my mother—all
her illnesses
still intact—leans
her softnesses
over my crib,

and tries with-
out words to
hold me. She
tries and tries
to hold me.

OUTLOOK

Lying flat, under a green machine
hung from the ceiling's crossed tracks,
its big crayon-tip aimed at my guts,

I can read its big nameplate: PICKER.
Up from the box the tip comes out of,
three $1/2$" cables, flexibly tied to each other,

climb in long half-loops up a green arm
to the ceiling, before heading out
to wherever they get their power. Which

comes down them into the box, out through
the crayon's nose-cone, through me and
the table I'm flat on, onto film

in a lightproof tray. Two of the cables
look lighter gray than the third. And slightly
kinked, where black marks show the remains

of electrical tape before the advent
of serrated plastic ties. Which now
bind in the dark third, the part

they had to replace to make the whole
machine work: so they could look into
whatever's next, whatever it is I'm in for,

here lying flat as the film that, as
it develops, will show what doesn't appear
out under plain old sky.
                              Sky. Which when I
came in, was just beginning to snow.

HAND

In sheer pain, or
desperate to hurt,
it self-clenches;

reshaped to cleave,
tensed hard, it
can strike down.

A child's, taught,
will stretch palm
nearly flat, to give

an apple to a pony.
A man's, wrist back,
palm down, can try

to push self up,
thinking to push
gravity away.

Anyone's, held
naturally, palm
up, cups all

it can't contain:
the frequencies of
light, the weightless

breath of air it
breathes, kinds
of wonder that

the body opens
to embody. It's
true. Hold out

your left, rib-
high, to sky:
feel it fill.

Or know, eyes
closed, it is
already full.

ALBA

A slit of streetlight, angled
on the wall. This side of dream,
waking, I stretch across a time zone to
another state, to you
not yet woken:
                    how your neck
uncovers when your shoulder
wanders, your lips happy
even in sleep; how, displacing
cold, your toes reshape the dark.
The delta and the highlands of
your South, the soft high and
low weight of one breast turning
to the other;
                    as waking, each to
each from there and here, we toward
each other turn, how gentle from how far
your hands:
                    long dear, how deep you reach.

SIXTY-THREE

Man I thought I knew well,
feeling his age, asked me
outright, *What do you believe?*

I thought of my daughter
in her hard time, who
learned, between her mouth

and cupped hands, to sound
the prime call of a loon.
I could have said trees,

oaks with fog in them, grown
from split rock next to tides.
I might have said dayrise,

November sun. Or the bow-wave tune
a sailboat plays in light air.
I thought of my daughter

in her hard time; the turn
of the solstice, the way
words find for how life feels.

I know, I said, *without love
there's no music. No music left
to lift hard weathers, to lend*

*old courage its great gift:
to keep believing in love.* From far
in the dark of a lake, the shape

of my daughter's voice got to me:
I told myself *I have to believe.*
Courage takes love and gives.

CHANCES

As whitecaps ride
mid-ocean swells, and
tumble on themselves,

love's moved to love:
love praises love, proud
of its quick gravity;

love loves to spend its
gifts, gives silence
time, lets hummings

turn to music. Love takes
its chances, touches lightly,
dances to the tune it just

invented. Unannounced,
love pounces on its luck,
lives in eyes alive with

its grave levity. Various
in word, in deed, love,
countless times a day, says

yes. Love knows the names
the other loves, reads
the other's sense of every

tree, cove, sky; in its
flurries, even furies, love's
transformative; while waves

reshape the beaches where they end,
love remains the mystery
love, in us, informs.

REAWAKENING IN NEW ENGLAND

In a house twice older
than I am, a man closing
on seventy, newly
recovered from going
half blind, I'm
home;
      up before
sunup, still dreaming
three women, my back
braced by the grace
of an Eames chair,
I'm here:
      reunited
with Chekhov, living
in books, feeling
for words, revising
this poem;
      here's
where I am, up
against odds,
      having
an ardent dawn.

FOG-TALK

Walking the heaved cement sidewalk down Main Street,
I end up where the town bottoms out: a parking lot
thick with sea-fog. There's Wister, my boyhood friend,

parked on the passenger side of his old Dodge pickup.
He's waiting for Lucia, the girl who drives him around
and feeds him, the one who takes care of him at home.

Wister got married late. Wifeless now, no kids, he's near
sixty-eight. Like me. Watching the ebb, looking out into
the fog. Fog so thick that if you got shingling your roof

you'd shingle three or four courses out onto
the fog before you fell off or sun came. Wister knows
that old joke. Not much else, not any more. His mind drifts

every whichway. When I start over to his old pickup,
he waves to my wave coming toward him, his window half up,
half down. He forgets how to work it. I put my head

up close. *Wister,* I say, *you got your compass with you
to steer her home through this fog?* Wister smiles at me with
all sorts of joy, nodding yes. He says *I don't know.*

SEVENTY

Zero out the kitchen
window. Up 2° from
noon. *Too cold for snow,*

we used to say. The radio
says flurries. Our bones
know better now, our noses

smell the metal sky.
By three, a big low
off the coast; we know

its January weight.
Power lines down. Whorls
of horizontal snow.

At iron dusk, the white-out.
No other house in sight.
Drifted beyond compass,

we light two candles, bank
the woodstove, move up stairs.
In this barely anchored bed

we let our legs warm up
our feet. Which mingled, heat
the rest of us against

the deep old dark. All night
the constant roar: as we once
dove from rocks to swim, we

let old waves wash over us,
waves like this storm,
fetched from a far shore.

X

LONG AFTERNOONS IN DAKOTA

Some plainly hot.

Lala, a Pakistani long in Grand Forks,
much given to early American sea-chests, takes
out her Leica, her eyebrows showing over the lens
she has fixed

next door on

Don J., a forty-year ponytail boy who shifts his eye,
view-finding through his new Nikon, onto
a poet's spaniel named Peekaboo, a yard-dog
with limited focus;

none of whom

entertain for a minute the non-Euclidian triangle
they—without posing—compose: they proceed, if
at all, by long fractions of seconds, adjusting
their film speeds or shutters

to June afternoons

in Grand Forks, where I've never been, except to
picture them, cropped, stopped down to f. 16, their local
depth of field, through which they move with a slowness
of music I don't quite remember,

probably by Hovhaness.

LIFETIMES

A day,
        close to each other's
winter solstice: two lives,

halfway between pole and
equator, ranging the coast's

granite edge. Kept feeling
the ebb tide starting to turn.

Climbed an ice-age boulder; sat,
to be done with tuna on rye.

Gathered themselves, waded in
lightly. Playing ripples, let

waves overcome them. Each, knee-
deep, lifted each to touch sky.

Turned back ashore. Within hemlock
and hardwood, found a glade soft

with December sun. Sun they'd been
waiting for
                thirty-two years.

HOT 5TH OF JULY

A housepainter ladder'd up
on a white clapboard house.
Out on the street, across
the lawn from its Toro rider,
a T-shirt kid, scrawny, maybe
thirteen or eleven, parked
in the rusted-out box
of an old Dodge Ram. Must
be his boy, maybe serving
a sentence. Or not all there.
Hard to know. Hunched up on
the wheelwell, his body slumps,
his eyes scan nothing. He
sits there, hot hot hot, all
morning, diddling a piece
of trash from the box, then
sticking his mid-finger up
his nose. Head bent, no cap,
waterjar empty or never
filled, he slumps there, beyond
choice or prospect. Only
wishing, one of these times,
his old man might get down,
let him out, let go,
let him scream the Toro
around the scorched lawn.

VIEWS

Waking, you thumb the remote
to scan news,
             watch the weather girl
dance both hands, pivot,
smile, and point to
             the other coast.
So what does morning look like?
What does the world.
             From this motel:
an anywhere town, across the bay, shining.
Elsewhere mountains.
             Miles beyond hills,
the capital cities, their walls behind walls.
Monuments to our lies,
             to our self-blinded lives.
Above us now, two fishhawks, cheeping musical shrieks,
the risen sun easing their wingbeats.
             Over us all,
daylight's invisible satellites, shamelessly
bouncing back from space the emptiness we feed them.

LATE WAKINGS

This is the gray of it.
                Even the house.
All its everythings so much nothing.
Far from what we believed it once meant.
Every mail tries to sell elsewhere: offers
of off-season discounts, countless folders
of equatorial beaches, condos, and sun.
Here the gales, steely weathers, sleet.
Aside from the sun, nothing we've longed for.
Predators overhead, hawks dying to stoop.
Scavenging gulls, ravens, working the street.
Everywhere, where we apparently live, fear.
Anger on narrowing edges. We wake from nightmares
to nightmare newscasts. So it's morning again,
again.
        All day the sky's smearing up.

RECALLINGS

After his father's
fourth wife phoned
before dawn, said

his Dad fell out of
their bed, couldn't
quite talk, it looked

like a stroke, he
knew he'd have to
go. God, she'd said,

the ambulance guys
took him straight to
the big new wing

of Mid-State Medical
Center, where she
then was, but was

going to work soon.
He drove all day:
once started out of

the Adirondack dark, he
bridged the Hudson,
carved curves across

the grain of Green
Mountains and White;
then Maine, his head

newly full of his
Old Man's failings.
It was dark again

by the time he got
there. The new wing
elevator suddenly

shorted out. No sign
of Gwen. The nurse,
talking embolism or

hemorrhagic leaks,
walked him up into
the semi-private where

his father lay solo.
Lay strapped down, bed-
rails up, an IV in

his arm, his face like
putty. He reached
for his father's hand,

found that that opened
his eyes, and gave
his father to say

the single sentence he
that night spoke. Spoke
the sentence his son,

being tunnelled into
a CAT-scan in another
century, would out

of nowhere recall:
I, his father slowly
professed, *must have*

*the smallest penis
in the whole
world.*

THE MAN WHO LOST HIS WIFE

Words get to him now. They leap out of
second grade schooldays, when big kids

bullied him to point his pistol finger at
his temple, then made him yell *M T!*

These days he can't forget his novel,
Death on the Mississippi, a looseleaf

of blank pages he every night rewrites.
If his radio's preset alarm goes off,

the weather girl gets to him every time
she claims today is going to be *fair.*

When he goes back, too late, to bed,
he hears himself *repair* thereto.

His head's an echo chamber: he feels,
come Fall, the house in *disrepair.*

What hurts most is how unanswerably
the words show up. Words come out of

children's closets. Words that make up
sentences; letters cracked-plaster spell

on the stairwell wall, raw words
he cannot bear. Swept downstream long since,

her voice still tells him all he knows.
Everything means something else.

AN OLD AIRMAN WHO KNOWS WHO HE WAS

In the light of twelve-o'clock-high
I'm on most days safe.
                    Now, playing
centerfielder in the black third hour
beyond midnight, assaulted by Day-Glo balls
arc'd at me by batters all over the infield,
my head comes half-off.
                    ***
                    The old fear
climbs inside my bared skull,
                                        sinks
into my gut, freezes me
with how old it is.
                    Scrunched,
trying to lift myself up, I'm again
my own victim, my mind dizzied by
self-designated hot batters, big kids
dreaming all night their dreams
of watching me drop.
                    ***
                    In the time it takes
for my right brain to figure what's going
to happen, my left hand goes numb, the stars
burn out, my eyes roll up toward
the back of my head.
                    Wherever I move,
those sons-of-hitters, invaders tough
as the old Gashouse Gang, whack fungoes
all over the ballpark.
                    ***

That park was my boyhood place,

                               my own

backyard. Every Opening Day

                          I kept

singing my guts out,

                    singing

The Star Spangled

                 you know.

           ***

                So back
I've come, close to Baltimore, fifty-some
autumns this side of Pearl Harbor, D Day,
Victory-in-Somewhere-Day, the Bomb, or

my country Right-or-Wrong Day. Here, not quite
at attention, *sans* cap, in GI khakis,
a Pfc stripe on both sleeves, my chest

full of ribbons: the Good Conduct,
the Georgia Theatre of Operations,
a Pair Medal with Lipstick Clusters,

and one Purple Heart.

               ***

                Just last week
the VA shrink got so low he told me
I'm down to admitting I want to be battered.
Said Day-Glo balls were my rockets' red glare,
said I'd been waiting lifelong for me or
the world to grow up or blow up.

                     I said

Maybe I'm baby Moses,

               already warmed up

in the bullpen,

              His head shook it off, said

he'd double my meds beginning next week. But
he didn't, at least not yet.

***

Every

bad night the batters keep coming,
the field sinks and swells, up-
heaving my life.

Some days I think

I'm part of the New World's new
World Series, forever amounting
to Zilch-to-Zilch.

Shiver'd

all over, sphincters gone,
I only know I'm trying
to hang in there.

***

I'm already

zeroing-in on the rest of my life.
It's getting that time.

Near time for

Doc Zwink's stud nurse to march in like
reveille, his GI tray full of meds in
GI cups. Like reveille early in '43,
back in tarpaper barracks in plain old
Greensboro Basic: *Ev-reebody up! Let go
your cocks and grab your socks.* . . .
Already it's coming on six, already
false dawn. Me, I'm warmed-up all right,
set to figure how this time
I'll get to him.

Who knows?

Who knows

how that bastard will yell
when he finally finds me.

COMING TO

Coming to woods in light spring rain,
I know I am not too late.
                          In my week
of walking down from White Mountains,
I dreamt I might die before
familiar woods woke me.
                          Come slowly,
the way leaves come, I've arrived at
their turnings: from bronze, gold, wine,
to all greens, as they let sun in
to tug them toward light.
                          Come again now
to woods as they've grown, hardwood
and soft, birch, hemlock, and oak,
I walk into my boyhood,
                          back to
my mother,
            the mother who took me in hand
to steer me across back fields to the woods.
Over and over, she slowed to give me
the local names: swampmaple, shadblow,
hackmatack, pine.
                    Given those woods,
trees renewed in me now, I've begun
to know I'm older than all
but the tallest stands.
                          Under trees,
I discover my mother's old namings
beginning to bloom: bloodroot,
hepatica, bunchberry, trillium;
                          in air

so quiet the flowers barely move,
I shiver a little, over and over.
I listen to trout lily, violet, jack-
in-the-pulpit, spring beauty.

I let my head bow as I name them.

WRITING IT DOWN

Was an old man, no
jazz left. No doubt
about it, tired as

Hell. Fell asleep
early, woke somewhere
near two. Mostly woke

screamless, half-awake
quick. Felt for his
pretty ones, found his

wife took them. Flown
on his ticket, flown
long since. He stormed,

bare as Lear, thought
cogito, ergo. . . . Grabbed
for the ballpoint next

to his bed. Steered
his blind thumb down
tonight's spiral note-

book, came up with slant-
wise words in the dark.
By daybreak saw them:

I'm afraid as I am.
Whatever they meant
he stayed wed to

their presence. Sank
back toward sleep, flat
as a flounder. Recalled

how his last book got
remaindered. Re-remembered
the spider-webbed world,

which snatched out of print
the old language of trees.
No wonder now; no one

of a mind to ponder
how meanings dance.
Odds were against him.

A mere five words.
A pre-posthumous poet's
raw self-sentence.

AGELESS MINUTES

Having, for nearly an hour,
given him Therapeutic Massage
and Reiki Healing, she lays

both hands on the cotton sheet
over the old man's solar plexus.
Lastly, now, she first lifts

her palms, then fingertips,
as he hugely exhales. As if
by stopwatch, the New Age music

clicks off. Close to the bench,
still, she stands silent for
a deep moment, then leans

toward his bared right shoulder
to whisper *There you are.* . . .
And so exits. His eyes remain

closed. Not yet ready to
get up or dress, he lets
his body exult. His grin

reflects on the ceiling,
sunstruck: it tells him
You're here, still here.

IDENTIFICATION

Morning routine at my desk.

Close to noon, a half-inch
insect, to me looking female,

starts up the high inside pane
of the Northeast window. Three

light yellow legs angle out
each side of her body; white wings

stay folded. Now she tries flight
for two inches; her dark feelers

signal to stop. I stand up
to figure her arrowhead head,

bright red; then two black bars,
a minuscule equal-sign, athwart

the aft-end of her abdomen. Given
another state, under another sky,

a native trout might well rise
to feed on such finite grace.

I know too well—I lost her
as I sank back, trying words

for us both. Hooked, still, I
long to identify what we're

about. In whatever sphere we've
arrived, I have to believe

we're met by meaning or chance.
Or both. How else can I think?

How validate wonder? Here, as I've
been sounding my luck in noon light,

that luminous she-creature, barely
moments ago, reappeared on this page,

the page on which I now write.

WITHIN

A peninsula church, October's last Sunday.
Outside, a half-gale. Barely beyond the twelve-
over-twelve high panes of the Southwest window,

frost-paled maple leaves, still stemmed to
their half-stripped tree, stream a bright translucence.
Sunstruck, cloudstruck, horizon-bound by

the seawind, they outshine the sermon, the hymns,
the words of the congregation's oldest prayer.
Given the leaves' light, their benediction, matched

by the Bach *partita* fallen or risen to us through
its thousand seasons, we feel our lives bare: without
guilt or reason, we let our eyes fill and be lifted.

NARROW ROAD, PRESIDENTS' DAY

As I drive by
the architect's
house, his wife's

just opening up
the sideyard window
and leaning out

on her elbows to
talk with three
backyard sheep.

She smells spring.
Given sun trying
to break through

dawn fog, fog after
all-night rain, on
top of two months

of old snow, she
gives herself
gasps of light.

Not a mile back,
just beyond Harman's
Farm Stand, all

boarded-up against
winter, almost at
the new place where

they sell Russian
tractors, I sniffed
skunk, first time

this year. Had to
swerve my pickup
to keep from side-

swiping the skunk,
already dead. And
next to him, for

Christ's sake, a big
mother porcupine,
dying hard.

I kept on driving
to work. I keep
on now, holiday

or no, my whole
morning messed up
by road-kill, wannabe

Presidents, street
bombs, cyberspace,
Bosnia, and what's to

become of the former
United States, an
America only once

divisible. Half-
blinded by freeflow
tears and new sun,

I find myself
still touched by
the woman talking

with sheep. I try
to figure what they
say to each other;

and when, if spring
happens, the new
lambs will come.

REACH ROAD: *IN MEDIAS RES*

A roadside field, shielded
on three sides by woods.
Last fall a small meadow.
Now March, in noon sun,
a small snowfield, bright
as a high arctic summer.
Deep in glanced light,
old stonewalls tumble
through conifers, back
in woodlots without
a leaf left, far from
October's gold leaves
that blind a man, or tug
him toward May's first
green to replay Eden.

*

Driving Reach Road along
a stillness of snow,
the old Mailman on
his Rural Mail Route
keeps his weather-eye
out for views newly
deep. Bared hardwoods'
barred shadows, raw
woodsroads leading
to last winter's slash.
The still frozen marsh.
A slumped barn. Steeped
in new light, the North
bank of a West-running
brook gets high sun to

melt it. Roots expose:
a family graveyard, iron-
fenced, is alight amid
a caucus of crows.

*

Given his fifty-
week six-day-job,
after thirty years
of learning by
teaching, small wonder
that through tri-focals,
the Mailman both watches
the road and searches
for meaning, reading
the equinoctial woods.
Yet keeping going
he routinely stops,
starts, stops, drives left-
footed, thoughtlessly
steers with his left hand
to let himself lean
his right hand out
the righthand window to
put today's mail into
the right rural box.

*

Whatever the weather,
or hours lost to sleep,
he every day, for sake
of his soul, lifts down
a book from his highest
bookshelf: Emerson's
Journals, Rachel Carson,
Carruth or Jeffers;
Roethke, Eudora Welty,

Frost; Hawking's *Brief
History*, and *Endgame*.
He believes, without
prayer, in an ongoing
universe: Reach Road
not least, as the Sun
—systematically
solo as an old
Mailman—appears to
see to it that Earth,
both spinning and
tilting, continually
keeps its appointed
Grand Rounds. Consoled
as he is by orbits
and constellations,
he keeps at heart
the burdensome time
between Thanksgiving
and Christmas: long days
of short light. Nights
weighing the more as
they measure the years
since his single sister's
slow December death.

*

Come September, there
still are evenings
when he keeps driving
into the dark on
automatic pilot.
Yet given today,
given sun to space,
he lifts his whole life
toward high June, the hemi-

sphere's season of lives
returning to wildwoods,
salt tides: the roadside
Edenic with daisies,
buttercups, clover.
High Season, too, for
Bostonian generations:
migrating again to
inherit white-clapboard
houses, shingle cottages,
tennis courts, sailboats,
island picnics, informal
gardens brilliant as
Northwest-wind days.

*

Homing his Jeep Wagoneer
through its March rounds in
equinoctial light, he
eases toward early supper,
reclaiming the sense
an old summer poet
once told him: something
like *Life consists of*
propositions about
its very self. Washing
dishes, he happily
figures that, save for
the leaves, an evening
next September will
closely mirror today's
slants of light. So
self-informed, stepping
outside to relieve
himself, he checks for
first stars and planets.

He quiets. Yet even
before he sinks into
bed, he starts dreaming
June's dreamy teen-age
daughters, swarming
every high noon around
their familiar Rural
Route boxes. Gigglingly
waiting for boy-mail
(postmarked the like of
Concord, Lincoln, Milton,
Brookline or Chestnut Hill),
they dance barefoot, their
body language already
encoding their laughter.
Mailman ever, barely
asleep, he smiles to
himself the smiles
the girls give him when
he delivers. Moonstruck
already, now that Earth
spins him to snore, he
finds himself wishing,
on every star, returns
from his first kissings.

*

Three-hundred-and-sixty-
some days a year, he
wakes in the dark. Well
before sun-up, he feels
his heart stretching,
embracing pure morning.
Today he begins by
returning the *what-cheer
what-cheer* whistle of

a lone cardinal. Then
he opens to whatever
page of his bedside
Walden. After break-fast,
ritual ablutions, he
checks the barometer,
steps down into the barn,
and sidles up to his
faithful Jeep, as if
this was Horsepower Farm.
Routinely, he swipes
his left sleeve over
three capital words on
the driver's ridged door:
TIME'S WINGED CHARIOT,
the motto he painted on
his first truck, and all
after. Which marvel
reminds him about
the Mexican poet
who said *Light is time
thinking about itself.*
Timely, ever, he starts
his new chariot up
over Sedgwick Ridge
toward the Blue Hill P.O.;
where, before seven, he
must sort the mail-load
he's bound to deliver
all along old Reach Road.

                    *

Shifting gears again
up the barren ridge,
navigating toward
the small mountain

that gave name to
the town, he misses
last week's splendid
Snowy Owl, likely
flown to its summer
tundra. Thinking time
and place in his own
life, he recollects
that Thoreau, three
half-centuries ago,
thought he might be
a mail-carrier in Peru.

*

Driven down Blue Hill's
Tenney Hill, Peru aside,
he finds time to stop in
at Partridge Drugs for
his herbal tea, sitting
with coffee drinkers
at Maine's longest Soda
and Snack Bar, the usual
gossip going full tilt.

*

Five minutes more. Drives
two hundred feet, stops
at the clapboard front
of the P.O., backs down
to the loading platform.
Before he climbs up
the six granite steps
to start sorting, he
stretches from neck down,
his feet at the edge of
Blue Hill's inner harbor,
sun shimmering against

the ebb of the tide.
Cleaning his glasses,
he tries to figure
how, on such mornings,
he has, over nineteen
years, been his own man.
Signed on for one more,
weathers and tides not
withstanding. He asks
himself *How can
one love,
love life without
the pondering.* Confused,
he starts up the stairs,
gets his left-foot half-
up on step five, which
twists him backward as
gravity tugs him down to
hard ground, lying there
next to his Jeep. They
say Thayer Hatch got to
him first, yelled back
to the mailroom to go
for help. Aside from
putting a big coat
over him, there wasn't
much help. Not until
the town ambulance came.

*

Came it did, red lights
flashing, two on-call
EMTs, a volunteer
driving. All calm as
could be, once they found
the scene safe. Took his

pulse and his airway,
started IV, though his
bleeding was superficial.
Let his eyes answer
their questions. Played
safe with a collar,
strapped him onto
a longboard and lifted
him into the litter.
Transported him in
supine position, back up
to Partridge Drugs; hooked
a quick left, and two
quick rights, into
the Ambulance Entrance
at the town hospital.

*

Once they'd rolled him
inside, under familiar
cover, interns, nurses,
in the ER took over.
Checked him inside and
out, his head full of
stars, altogether
too woozy to figure.
Long after noon he
finds he's flat out in
bed, a young LPN
checking the slow IV,
her hand soothing his
forehead and neck. When
the fine new doctor
came back from her day-
conference Downeast,
he hears without memory

that the CAT-scan was
clear, that his buttocks
saved all bones but his
left big toe. She said
what probably happened
was a Syncopic Episode,
likely an irregular heart-
beat; *i.e.* a blackout.
Told him he'd be home
in a day or two. Exit
this wonder; old Mailman
drifts off, heart beating
to Roethke's iambics:
I wake to sleep and
take my waking slow.
Beyond midnight, as
a new nurse shows up,
he says it again,
and sleepily adds
to her, and himself,
I learn by going
where I have to go.
When she leaves, he
mumbles his nightly
Augustinian prayer:
Night shall release
its splendor that
morning shall appear.

*

Appear it did, through
the Northeast window,
his curtain open wide,
thanks to the recent
night nurse. With tri-
focals busted, no

need for a bedside
Walden. Yet his eyes
sufficiently clear to
see Old Sol pretend
to climb up over
a far horizon. Thus
does a Mailman get
to play the Thoreau
he knows by heart: *Only*
that day dawns to which
we are awake. There
is more day to dawn.
The sun is but
a morning star.

*

Gospel well taken,
he means to seize
the day: first scanning
across the inner
harbor to Sea Side
Cemetery; then over
gravestones, he lifts
his eyes up unto
Blue Hill Mountain:
a bedrock mound, long
anchored under the
Laurentide ice-sheet.
Marvelling, he re-
members Geology I:
the ice, some fourteen-
thousand years back,
began to melt and
recede, the salt sea
following inland;
whales, seals, into Maine

bays. Land, in another
three thousand years, re-
bounding: Paleoindians
migrating from West and
South, camping below
the edge of the glacier,
their spearpoints ready
for mammoth and caribou,
searching grasslands under
the honking of snow geese.
Merged out of chaos
through hospital glass,
he wonders clearly
how creatures began
to approach, or re-
proach, who we have
seemed to become.

AGAIN, THE SOLSTICE

Still.
A stillness.
Not a storm's eye

or its afterlife.
Not the closed quiet
of fog. Only this

high June sky, far
inland, its five
clouds stilled,

the long light
evening. Rooted,
some hundred feet

from the back lot's
hundred-foot pine,
the two of us,

immersed in time
with the tree,
open ourselves to

be touched by light,
light becoming
and gone, gone

and becoming. Moved,
under the tree's
tall stillness,

we let our lives,
lived at groundlevel,
heighten; as the

planet starts to
tilt back toward
dark, we see

how light informs
the tree: at the
utmost tip of its

every branch, the tips,
only now, are just
beginning to candle.

PASSAGE WITHOUT RITES

Homing, inshore, from far off-soundings.
Night coming on. Sails barely full.
                                    The wind,
in its dying, too light to lift us against
the long ebb.
                    My two fingers, light
on the tiller, try to believe I feel
the turned tide.
                    Hard to tell. Maybe,
as new currents pressure the rudder,
I come to sense
                    the keel beginning
to shape the flow of the sea. Deep
and aloft, it's close
                    to dark.
No stars yet. Only the risen nightwind,
as we tack into its warmth,
                                    tells us
we'll make our homeport. Strange,
angling into the dark,
                    to think
how a mainsail's camber reflects
the arc of the keel,
                    their dynamics
reversing whenever we tack.
You call from below,
                    hand up coffee,
check the glow of the compass, and
raise an eye to Arcturus,
                    just now
beginning to shine. All over again,

all over, our old bodies
                      breathe
the old mysteries: the long night
still to go, small bow-waves
                           playing
a little *nachtmusik;* stars beyond stars
flooding our inmost eyes.
                      And voices,
now, come out of the dark,
deeply sounding our own.

ACKNOWLEDGMENTS

The jacket of *Lifelines* is a section of the mid-1850s Fitz Hugh Lane painting of "Blue Hill, Maine," which comes from a private collection and is here reproduced by the kind permission of its owners.

Thanks again to editors of the following journals for first printing these poems of the past five years, some in versions now slightly revised:

The American Poetry Review: "Narrow Road, Presidents' Day," "The Man Who Lost His Wife"; *The Amicus Journal:* "Within"; *The Beloit Poetry Journal:* "Reach Road: *In Medias Res*"; *DoubleTake:* "Long Afternoons in Dakota," "Recallings"; *Five Points:* "Ageless Minutes"; *The Georgia Review:* "Late Wakings," "Views"; *The Kenyon Review:* "An Old Airman Who Knows Who He Was"; *North Dakota Quarterly:* "Hot 5th of July"; *The Ohio Review:* "Again, the Solstice"; *Poetry:* "Coming To," "Writing It Down"; *Shenandoah:* "Identification"; *The Southern Review:* "Lifetimes"; *The Yale Review:* "Passage Without Rites."

Most of all, this millennial book
of lifetime poems is dedicated to
the seven grandchildren ever more
deeply a part of our lives and love:

Will	Purnima	Caroline
Joseph	Malcolm	Anne
	and Christian	